LODESTONES

Lodestones

NEW POEMS WRITTEN IN CELEBRATION
OF TWELVE POETS FROM AROUND THE WORLD

EDITED BY

Roger Garfitt

THE BORDER POETS · 2001

Front cover, clockwise from top centre:
Georg Trakl, Osip Mandelstam, James Baxter,
Guillevic, Maxine Kumin, Rolf Jacobsen.
Drawing © Rita Carter 2001

The collection © 2001
The Border Poets
The Community College, Bishop's Castle

The copyright of individual items belongs to the contributors

First published 2001
by The Border Poets, The Community College
Bishop's Castle, Shropshire SY9 5AY

ISBN 0-9524080-2-3

Photoset in 10.5 on 13 pt Mergenthaler Sabon
at Five Seasons Press, Hereford
and printed on Five Seasons recycled paper
by Biddles Ltd, Guildford and King's Lynn

LEGAL NOTICE

All rights reserved. No part of this book may be reproduced, stored in a retrieval systems or transmitted in any form, or by any means, electronic, mechanical, photocopy, recording or otherwise without permission from The Border Poets, c/o The Community College, Bishop's Castle.

Requests to publish work from this book must be sent to The Border Poets, The Community College, Bishop's Castle, Shropshire SY9 5AY.

The contributors have asserted their rights under section 77 of the Copyright, Designs and Patents Act 1988 to be identified as the authors of this work.

British Library Cataloguing in Publication Data.
A catalogue record of this book is available from the British Library.

Contents

Introduction   7

Acknowledgements   8

Epigraph (Bryan Podmore)   9

Guillevic   11
Brenda Lealman 12; Christopher Allan 13; Brenda Lealman 14; Charles Johnson 15; Roger Garfitt 15; Rita Carter 16; Charles Johnson 17; Christopher Allan 17; Michael Henry 18

Maxine Kumin   19
Christopher Allan 21; Amanda Attfield 23; Rita Carter 24; Caroline Gourlay 26; Rita Carter 27; Miranda Tite 29; Charles Johnson 30

Rolf Jacobsen   31
Roger Garfitt 32; John Harrison 32; Bryan Podmore 33; Christopher Allan 34; Miranda Tite 35; Michael Henry 36; Brenda Lealman 37; Tricia Torrington 38; Brenda Lealman 39; Rita Carter 41

James K. Baxter   43
Roger Garfitt 45; Christopher Allan 46; David Hart 47; Roger Garfitt 48; Rita Carter 49; John Harrison 51; Brenda Lealman 52, 53; Gavin Hooson 54

dom silvester houedard   55
Christopher Allan 57; Charles Johnson 58; Christopher Allan 59; David Hart 60; John Harrison 61; Caroline Gourlay 62; John Harrison 62; Amanda Attfield 63; Bryan Podmore 64; Richard Beaumond 64

Juan Ramón Jiménez   65
Christopher Allan 66; John Harrison 67; Tricia Torrington 68; David Hart 69; Tricia Torrington 70; Miranda Tite 70; Roger Garfitt 71; Michael Henry 72

Contents *(continued)*

Eugenio Montale — 73
David Hart 74; Christopher Allan 75; Michael Henry 76; Rita Carter 77; Michael Henry 78; Tricia Torrington 79; Rita Carter 80; John Harrison 82; Amanda Attfield 84; Roger Garfitt 85; Rita Carter 85; Bryan Podmore 86

Georg Trakl — 87
Christopher Allan 88; Miranda Tite 89; Michael Henry 89; Rita Carter 90; David Hart 91; Trevor Innes 92; Charles Johnson 94

Osip Mandelstam — 95
Amanda Attfield 96; David Hart 97; John Harrison 98; Trevor Innes 99; Richard Beaumond 101; Christopher Allan 102

Derek Walcott — 103
Brenda Lealman 105; Gavin Hooson 106; Rita Carter 106; John Harrison 109; Miranda Tite 111; Roger Garfitt 111; Michael Henry 112

Rabindranath Tagore — 113
Michael Henry 114; Brenda Lealman 114; Christopher Allan 115; John Harrison 116; Trevor Innes 117; David Hart 117; Eleanor Cooke 118

Yehuda Amichai — 119
Gavin Hooson 120; Charles Johnson 120; Rita Carter 121; David Hart 122; Ursula Freeman 123; Christopher Allan 124; David Hart 125; John Harrison 125; Roger Garfitt 126

Biographical Notes — 128

Introduction

There is a moment in 'Walking Bare', one of the poems in Ted Hughes's sequence, *Cave Birds*, when the protagonist looks beyond himself and realizes that he is

>a spark in the breath
>of the corolla that sweeps me.

That is rather the spirit in which the Border Poets undertook their millennial project, the series of workshops that have culminated in *Lodestones*. The energy pulse we call poetry, one expression of the energy pulse we call the universe, takes many different forms in many different languages. We tried to get some sense of the sweep of the imagination over the last century by looking at the work of twelve poets from around the world. Some, like Jacobsen and Jiménez, were founders of the modern movement. Some, like Amichai and Montale, brought new energies into the language, marrying colloquial vitality to the resonances of tradition. Some, like Mandelstam and Trakl, affirmed the imagination's power to survive and outlast the brutalities of history. And some, like Maxine Kumin and Derek Walcott, are continuing to create a poetry of celebration from the material of everyday life.

We did not draw up a master plan. We took it in turns to run the workshops, suggesting names as they occurred to us, poets from whom we drew energy for our own work, poets we felt, in David Hart's phrase, were on to something. We revealed our allegiances, surprised to discover how often we held them in common. David would have championed James K. Baxter if I hadn't. Michael Henry suggested Trakl and I was able to lend him a book from my shelves. These are the shaping spirits, the poets from whom other poets take their bearings, and, as we offer our work written in response to theirs, it seems only right to call the book *Lodestones*.

Clearly we do not accede to Paul Valéry's view that poetry is what is lost in translation. Anyone reading this book will sense that there were many moments when the imagination made contact. But there were moments when we floundered between conflicting translations, unable to find a firm footing in the dictionary. Such moments inspired Bryan Podmore's poem and it's a pleasure to open a challenging book with a light-hearted epigraph.

We are grateful to the National Lottery for the grant, awarded through the Arts Council of England, that funded the workshops and the publication of this book. And grateful, once again, to Robin Parish for the chance to hold the workshops in the unparalleled setting of Walcot Hall.

ROGER GARFITT

Acknowledgements

Almost all these poems were written in the course of the Walcot workshops or in response to the workshop material. A number have since been published and acknowledgements are due as follows:

Christopher Allan's 'Stone Mouth' and 'Teapot' first appeared in *Other Poetry*. 'Writing at Six Below', 'Letter from the Mountain', 'The Tao of the Keys', 'Broken Lines' and 'Poem' first appeared in *Fire*. 'Cracks' first appeared in *Pulsar*.

Amanda Attfield's 'A Few Seconds on the Callow' first appeared in *The Rialto*.

Roger Garfitt's 'A Chance of the Light' first appeared in an earlier draft in *London Magazine*, and then in his *Selected Poems*, published by Carcanet. His jazz poem, 'Mingus: Self-Portrait in Three Colours' was first performed with the John Williams Septet as part of the BBC's Music Live Weekend in May 2000.

Caroline Gourlay's 'Sam Unlimited' and 'Waiting' first appeared in her collection *Against the Odds*, published by the Hub Press.

Charles Johnson's 'The bruja Honda pretext' first appeared in an earlier draft in *Brando's Hat*.

Bottom, thou art translated

First watchword: Stay Alert!
See if they go changing words,
fuchsias to begonias, or
armadillos to anacondas,

and wonder if it is the moon
that's set serene upon the waves
or the sun become its substitute
smouldering above the desert

check if the text
has been darkened
or lightened
even asked
to
do
the splits.

Second watchword: Come Again?
Are they taking liberties, making
this foreigner sound English,
brought closer to our
pernicketiness?

For sure or certain or sooth
they come again to our deafness
with open or hidden agendas
give us another version in verse.

All so unsettling
when what we think
we wanted was
a stable clear rendition

without seven types of ambiguity.

BRYAN PODMORE

Guillevic
1907–1997

Though Guillevic wrote in French and spent his working life in the tax office in Paris, his poetry sprang from his Breton childhood, as is evident from his sequence *Carnac* (1961), which Bloodaxe have recently published in a new translation by John Montague. Guillevic saw the writing of *Carnac* as 'a deliverance. I recovered myself, my country, the earth and the sea; I relived everything that I had been.'

Earth and sea are fused in the title of his first book, *Terraque* (1945), a French adjective that fuses the Latin *terra* with the Latin *aqua*, Earthwatery, where English can only say Earthly. It was in *Terraque* that he wrote the first of his poems called simply '*Choses*', 'Things', poems that have fascinated me ever since I came across them in Savory's selection from Guillevic in *Penguin Modern European Poets*, now sadly out of print, though still to be found in libraries. They have an intense simplicity, an extraordinary concentration of feeling achieved through an extraordinary economy of means. He took that concentration even further in his *Euclidiennes*, poems based on the plainest of geometric shapes, where he is able to look, for example, at a circle and see

>   the motionless see-saw
>   nourishing you.

ROGER GARFITT

A nail

Only a little rust
on the nail.

It can't have been used yet.
It was taking it easy
like you or me.

It's one of those who have
gone quiet, gone
to look into themselves.

GUILLEVIC (from *Sphère*, 1963)
translated by Roger Garfitt

The Rhubarb Forcing Shed

is rooty, dark.
Nubbles of stems
grow throats.

You can hear me
snicking out of my sheath
as I come into the flitter

of candles and ruby brilliance,
the wax, bowed heads,
to and fro of the incantations:

Stockbridge Arrow
Cawood Delight
Rheum Palmatum
Appleton, Goliath,
Seedling Piggot, Rheum Ruby
Cawood Delight.

I was so eager to arrive:
the taste of earth,
plumped with shoddy.

But there are shadows
on the flitch beams, swinging
to the fullock in the soil.

Before I am broken off,
I would like to stand
in the light of the doorway

and look across the yard.

BRENDA LEALMAN

Stone Mouth

A guard of nettles
where a stream once was;
and grey dust, soft as sand.
Inside, spiders have found shelter
and spun and hung their targets.
Mouse or rat might root here
secret as spies. But under
this perfect arc, no arrowing
kingfisher comes; no dip
of any bird enters
the cool mouth of shadows
that is a tractor's grave.
Time has taken the wheel
and driven the beast into twilight.
Ironic, above its radiator,
the words, *Super Dexta*.
This is how the past
is garaged, how even the strength
of many horses
is finally pocketed and forgotten.
Does anyone now recall
the years when the spring floods
used to run swift
through this stone throat, emerging
like life to find the sun's heel?

CHRISTOPHER ALLAN

The Crack

I was on my way
to somewhere
across the kitchen floor.

You knelt beside me.
There is more than dust
down there, you said.

You made a draw tin
with the shovel
and yesterday's paper.

Through my opening
you drew the pent energy
of 300 million years.

Pulped tree ferns came up,
folds of eyelids,
fishy armours,

joints of horsetails,
scales, socketed stems
like backbones of a time to come.

From the wall
a shadow watched.
It shuddered as though wanting

to be blacked over,
to slip back into the before;
as though it would

have me blocked up,
stop me from seeing
how things could change,

would hold me back
from leaping into flame.
Burning is what I want.

BRENDA LEALMAN

Sticking up for cement

Will your paper dress
with the blue circle
keep you safe

when you go clubbing
with red builder's sand
your damp unpromising friend

both dreaming of being
sacks of ground oyster shells
water was leaving?

CHARLES JOHNSON

Isosceles Triangle

△

Feet planted square, it's not
your ground you stand
but your pace.

Honed edge, you cut
away any tie.

Still traveller,
you want to stay
light on your feet.

ROGER GARFITT

The Exhibit

It'll be ace, says her tousle-haired tutor in his red gingham
        shirt, eye inching over
the zinc plate balanced on his palms . . . Brick by brick she labours,
        incising into the early
hours, softening tone, monitoring distance, volume, shape, position,
        matching reference points,
taking early proofs, weakening and strengthening, assessing as the
        acid bit deeper into cuts;
inking up assiduously, caressingly mopping down, felting up her
        baby under the covers

before it slid under the old mangle-press, her elbow cranking the
        small wheel that drove
the larger till she peeled back the layers one by one like an
        artichoke . . . She waited
anxiously as they screwed up here, screwed down there, then
        exhausting their hanging
attempts, complaining that her TOWER was too high, they trailed
        her etching on the gallery
floor. . . But people will trample all over it!, she wailed . . . Exactly,
        their silence seemed to say.

RITA CARTER

The Burned Girl

The pale girl
in chef's check trousers
and white jacket
who came across to the shop

One cheek and one eye crumpled
by we guess a kitchen fat fire
but so pretty
withal

CHARLES JOHNSON

Teapot

When you rise each morning
I'm the first thing you reach for.

I belonged to your grandmother and I've been
the excuse for many conversations.

I'm getting old and have begun to dribble
but my tea is the finest you have tasted.

I was there when your mother got measles,
and when your father asked for her hand.

The day you were born they all had tea.
From all directions the cousins came.

Now my spout pours comfort into cups
as each funeral becomes a nail in your side.

CHRISTOPHER ALLAN

Masterclass with Guillevic

The women are taking notes.
It was always so. At University
they would scribble away in their long librarian skirts
while the men played Hit and Miss with memory.

Today in a masterclass on a Breton poet
you're writing down what I may come to rely on.
What I remember about Guillevic is anecdotal:
that he would take his hostess warmly by the breast.

Luckily there is no examination.
Only tomorrow morning, at ten o'clock,
you'll be sitting in front of a large desk
and a man will be taking notes.

MICHAEL HENRY

Maxine Kumin
born 1925

Maxine Kumin was brought up in Philadelphia and studied French and Russian at Radcliffe. She has taught in various universities and run writing workshops for Columbia, Brandeis and Princeton, but her poetry grows out of her life in New Hampshire, the life of a wife and mother, raising children, horses and vegetables. She is married to an engineering consultant and has two daughters and a son. She has published four novels and several children's books in addition to her poetry, for which she received the Pulitzer Prize in 1973.

I first came across her work in *The Bedford Introduction to Literature* by Michael Meyer, which includes her poem 'Woodchucks' as a demonstration of a poet's use of variety of tone. What knocked me out was the diction: spot-on, graphic and yet matter of fact. Plus, I must admit, the scheme, of regular end-rhymes, inconspicuous but perfect.

Seeking out more work of Maxine's, I found out how neglected she has been over here. She is mentioned in Diane Wood Middlebrook's biography of Anne Sexton, and I did manage to borrow a copy of her book of essays, *To Make a Prairie* (the title is from an Emily Dickinson poem), in which she quotes Richard Wilbur on the use of form: 'The strength of the genie comes from his being confined in a bottle.'

Maxine had become restless after the birth of her second child and made a pact with herself to sell a poem before the third was born. She did, and went on to publish regularly in magazines. Initially she specialized in light verse, influenced, among others, by Auden and MacNeice. In 1957 she began attending evening poetry workshops at Tuft's University, where she was teaching in the English Department, and met Anne Sexton. They discovered they were neighbours and exchanged phone numbers.

Daily dialogues soon developed, hours-long phone calls in which they would check each other's redraftings of poems. The 'extraordinary bond' that formed between them lasted until Anne's suicide in 1974. Early on they installed second phone lines, and would sometimes leave the phone off the hook, whistling when they were ready to resume. During Anne's periods of manic creativity, as when she was working on 'The Awful Rowing Toward God', she would be reading Maxine up to four new poems a day. All this for only eight dollars a month! Bouncing poems over the phone really does develop a poet's ear, Maxine says: for line breaks, for unintended internal rhymes, and for intended slant rhymes.

There is a glimpse of this intense relationship in Christopher Allan's 'Writing at Six Below', which also evokes the lives of two other New England poets, Hayden Carruth and Jane Kenyon. And I am very glad that we are able to open this section with one of the poems of Maxine Kumin's that I most admire, 'My Father's Neckties', reprinted by kind permission of the author.

CHARLES JOHNSON

My Father's Neckties

Last night my color-blind chainsmoking father
who has been dead for fourteen years
stepped up out of a basement tie shop
downtown and did not recognize me.

The number he was wearing was as terrible
as any from my girlhood, a time of
ugly ties and acrimony: six or seven
blue lightning bolts outlined in yellow.

Although this was my home town it was tacky
and unfamiliar, it was Rabat or Gibraltar
Daddy smoking his habitual
square-in-the-mouth cigarette and coughing
ashes down the lightning jags. He was
my age exactly, it was wordless, a window
opening on an interior we both knew
where we had loved each other, keeping it quiet.

Why do I wait years and years to dream this outcome?
My brothers, in whose dreams he must surely
turn up wearing rep ties or polka dots clumsily
knotted, do not speak of their encounters.

When we die, all four of us, in
whatever sequence, the designs
will fall off like face masks
and the rayon ravel from this hazy version
of a man who wore hard colors recklessly
and hid out in the foreign
bargain basements of his feelings.

MAXINE KUMIN

Writing at Six Below

Forests, snowfields, the moon drifting.
High farms that cling for life
to hill-curve in the north wind weather
fisting down from Canada.

Yet here in spring you see
a graze of heifers sunning in mild pastures
while an old grubber in jeans and shovel-beard
sweats to fix a worn-out McCulloch.

(2)

Carruth in northern Vermont
spent years observing his neighbours:
Johnny Spain, Marshall Washer, John Dryden,
and hammered from their likenesses
poems of humour and grit.

Wouldn't you too live up there
through a season of ice and dark
your hands calloused with work
your lower spine drumming
for a little of the gold he found?

(3)

Early morning, hunters polish rifles
in clouds of breath, dream of bears

on a mountain road, and disappear for hours
into the shadow-silences of trees,

their plain, spare spirits
having fingers lightly daring death

till it comes with a sudden movement
under a cloak of leaves yards ahead.

(4)

Kumin in New Hampshire
raising horses and writing.
Fall's brown and brass days
make way for months of blue ice.

She phones Anne Sexton
for the daily masterclass.
Slowly the miss-hit nails
ease out and true ones grip.
One day a raft of words duly launched
becomes the Henry Manly poems
and *House, Bridge, Fountain, Gate*.
Years later someone axes wood
an echo rings across ravines.
Each blow splits a wound wide.
Anne has called up nowhere
and become her own dark.

(5)

Your lids are heavy
you open a book
you open a door
and you are there at
Eagle Pond Farm.
The high slopes are snowbound.
A figure, far off,
walks her dog through drifts.
Already her blood is sick
already a silence takes her hand.
It's Jane Kenyon.
She disappears between
the under and the upper whiteness.
You follow her footprints for miles.
You might wake
at any time, hear
the snow-plough opening the lane
in a year she never had.

CHRISTOPHER ALLAN

A Few Seconds on The Callow

The first thing I knew was the thing cart-wheeling
toward us: a great black four-wheeled job
going wheels over roof, wheels over roof.
It's rubbish what they say about life flashing
before you. What flashed for me was 'It's a Shogun'
and I put my arms up, leaned across to the children.

I love those opera singers, the ones that take
forever to die, always front of stage, bosoms
heaving or bare, heads buried in their lover's
groin, and the breath-hold silence when the song ends,
pieces of it stuck like splinters in eyes and ears.
They get to die over again tomorrow.

The Shogun missed us. God knows how.
My mother claims her expert driving.
I guess I'll have to give her that one.
It came to a full stop, on its roof, half-buried in the hedge.
And we stopped. And I felt like that man
Roscoe Black who was laid on by a grizzly bear.

He said it just laid on him for a few seconds
and didn't do anything, he felt its heart beat next to his own.
He lived on. It was then I saw the second car
all punched-in at the back, its driver pulling and pushing at
    the door
and suddenly flames and splinters of car
flying up, falling every which way.

AMANDA ATTFIELD

The Great Escape

Remembered in my silent movies
my terrier dog Buster was so droll
                        like Keaton
you know, the way he narrowly escaped
                        disaster
through immaculate timing.

Keaton could clear a kitchen in a trice
jerking on a rope in one downward slice
to yank the whole tablemess skywards
                        the ceiling
catching it in one . . . then, tablelegs in air
above his head, he'd don hat with turned-up
                        brim,
the door clicking softly behind him, just as
                        a wall
collapses in thunderous dustclouds to miss
by a hair's breadth, while he steps
miraculously unharmed from the encircling
                        window-frame.

In the time it takes to carry plates from
                        table to sink
Buster could reach with his muzzle up & around
with the instinct of an experienced climber
negotiating an overhang, his teeth
                        clamping
softly around the remains of a leg of lamb
to snuck it into his basket without his
haunches leaving the blanket . . .

guarding it with teeth bared and a low growl
                        —such flair!

His corn-coloured curls were so soft like
                        Marilyn's
hair and his stare so innocent, contrite . . .

He lay doggo on our lawn on summer-long days,
resting his head on the pillow of his paws,
pretending to be content; turning around
every now and then, craftily, knowing
he was under surveillance . . .
as we turned away from the window, he'd
be flying through air, sweeping the gate

in one astounding leap, his tail flaming
                              the allotments
just when we thought him asleep.

He'd not come back for days and days, chasing
                              bitches
through woods, rivers . . .

I'd wake at four a.m. to a strange wolf-like wailing
at the back door, scold him, send him skulking
into the dark cave of his basket, swallowing
                              his tongue glibly . . .

or find him suddenly trotting along by the shops,
greeting me casually as a shopper.

One night, fearing him dead, so long was his
                              absence,
I prayed to a star for his return and was
                              amazed,
on opening my eyes, to find him bounding
up the garden path, filthy, stinking,
but not missing by a hair's breadth
                              to catch me
in one joyous leap.

RITA CARTER

Sam Unlimited

She sleeps unaware of being watched
her 'thereness' alters the balance of the room
her blackness holds the water of dreams,
one paw raised, air circles it slowly,
her tail, twitching slightly, feels the power of its curve
to and fro—walls tilt when she breathes.

The last of summer pours in through the window,
washes over the unmade bed.
Remembering a kill she is absent from the scene;
her bones long ago accepted flesh to
clothe an ancestry of silent currents that
cross and recross each time she stirs below
the surface of her muscled shoulders.

She sleeps lightly behind her eyes,
pebbles shifting in clear water;
a shudder ripples her layered fur . . .
Coming from a claimed territory,
coming from the bald, inhabited rocks,
coming from a landscape of hidden eyes,
back from the dark of her sleepless watch,
she yawns and stretches.

CAROLINE GOURLAY

Dad's Laughter

nor what handsprings are turned under
my ribs with winter gone
                    Maxine Kumin: Late Snow

It crazed Mum's face,
frozen in a photograph at a firm's dance,
vengeful at his thrown-back head,
laughing, triumphant.

His laughter was huge,
merciless, Rabelaisian.
It rouged cheeks, embarrassed neighbours,
caused me to suffer
tortures of suppressed giggles in church.

Steaming atmospheres intimate as kitchens
like a trembling valve on a pressure cooker
he whistled past my mother's tongue,
venting her displeasure through his joke.

It embraced landscapes,
blowing refreshing gusts into limp washing
as he strode out in gumboots to the allotments,
full-blown in the white sail of his vest.

Broad-backed, thick-set, limber-armed,
he coursed through dark waves of vegetables
like an aircraft carrier in the Atlantic,
dispersing the hovering rooks,
cutting swathes through cabbages, broccoli,
to split open the runner beans.

I climbed on to his shoulders,
floating on clouds of his laughter,
feeling the freedom and expanse of sky.
When I looked down, a young sailor gazed up,
smiling, swinging his kitbag,
home on leave from the war.

He was my conning tower,
eyes narrowed, scanning the horizon,
heartbeat a radar bleep
encircling the deep.

I was his tipping vessel,
gurgling, dark-deep, mirth-filled,
alone in my cot's dark cave
where he carried me from room to room
of my childhood, tapping my innocence
with a risk of enchantment.

His wheelbarrow bumping
the flightpath home through a sea of green,
a lightning flash gathers my father,

incandescent between splayed leaves
and pennants of scarlet beanflowers,

handsprings bursting winter
from the runnels of his ribcage
in chips of ice.

RITA CARTER

The blue rabbit

They gave me away
when I was thirteen months old
to a couple they hardly knew
who were hoping to adopt
and wanted a baby to practise on.

They reported that I would chant
*Give her rabbit, tuck her in,
turn the light off!* before they could
which they thought was sweet
and I think was sarcy.
Rabbit lived clamped to my side.

Months later I went home
with Rabbit.
My father's childhood friend
had just adopted a son.
They decided each to drive halfway
across the country to meet.
Parked in a hedgerow somewhere
peering into a carrycot
there was a whispered conversation.

They had no present
so they asked me to give the baby
my blue rabbit.
Horrified, I refused
and in rising anguish
was persuaded to obey.
I dropped the blue rabbit
towards the sleeping bundle
as though he was my blue-wrapped
heart and soul and guts.

Years later the boy, Alan,
came to stay and I adored him.
We took turns to push each other
in an old black pushchair
all around the streets.
He was my most perfect pal.
We were so bonded
I knew when we were grown
he would come back for me.

Then the cheerful letter
from his father:
Alan was getting married.
I had waited so long for him.
I can't believe he could do that to me.
If you read this, Alan,
I have just one message:
give me back my rabbit!

MIRANDA TITE

The bruja Honda pretext

I forget now upon what rococo alibi
the import of this bizarre
bramble-clad red
objet trouvé so much depends

how long ago bum up
its wheel-free front fangs
first knelt to pray their hungry
crayfish way into this hard
couchgrass-deep heart

and the arms of the young
Arthur Rackham shrub began
to claw round the hub
of the rear

O chrome, o aluminium!

It will for ever lunge, crashing
deep into the surf
a jet boat to transport
the soul of its rider
invisible Miranda
to the underworld

CHARLES JOHNSON

Rolf Jacobsen
1907–1994

Jacobsen was the first poet in Norway to relax the traditional verse forms, performing the equivalent of Pound's (much noisier) first heave: 'to break the pentameter, that was the first heave'. His open form and leaping image-associations have appealed to American poets such as Robert Bly (who translates Lorca, Machado and Neruda as well as Jacobsen) but are little known in Britain.

In the workshop we explored the relationship between 'meaning' and 'image' in a poem, considering the difference between a poem that aims to 'describe' something beyond itself (an 'experience' of the author, for example) and a poem which is no more than itself.

There are occasions, however, when Jacobsen appears to do both. He can open an argument and then clinch it with an image of such unexpected rightness that there is nothing more to be said. 'When they sleep' is complete as a world in itself: but it is a world that happens to contain our world.

GLENN STORHAUG

When they sleep

They are all children when they sleep.
There is no war in them.
They open their hands and breathe
in the slow rhythm given to humans by heaven.

Whether soldiers, statesmen, servants or masters
they purse their lips like small children
and most of them open their hands.
Stars stand watch then and the arch of the sky is hazed over
for a few hours when no one will harm another.

If only we could talk with each other then,
when hearts are like half-open flowers.
Words would push their way in
like golden bees
—God, teach me sleep's language.

ROLF JACOBSEN (*circa* 1953)
translated by Glenn Storhaug

Surfacing

The frog by the coal bunker
is breathing night
breathing the damp of it

a pear turning up the wick
of its lamp

a stone fresh from the sea
in its jacket of light

ROGER GARFITT

Stone

The builders have gone. Stone piled or scattered
Lies all around, roughens my hands,
Giving them strange sandpaper numbness
As, slowly arranging, I think of its origins
In silt and mud from blue-grey mountains,
Liquid in a shallow sea, layered
With skeletons of small sea-creatures
And settling near, so scientists say,
That part of the world which is now Uruguay.

Blue-grey slabs shed sudden wafers
Or smash into frost-begotten fragments
As though some deep desire compels them
To recover liquid freedom. With them lie
More robust pieces, paler, like pillows,
Lime mortar-encrusted as if by lichen,
Their latest provenance window spaces
We wanted in walls that darkly till now have
Surrounded two centuries' family life.

Deep-buried hulks resist exhumation
Like monsters with outsize secrets to guard,
That seem to betray long-forgotten walls
Or may have lain under a timber yard,
Its horses and wagons, sawdust and sweat,
And suddenly realization dawns
That in unthinking oil-fuelled freedom,
Slowly, self-taught, I am learning a skill
Older than history, as I build a retaining wall.

JOHN HARRISON

Tripod Rusting

Tripod, resting dilapidated
on an oaken stump, its turn well served
after long hours swung above the fire,
unembarrassed to show its age
in rings and crumbling cubes under saw.

Rested now, but not dismissing
the stir of rich stews it's nourished,
the apples bobbing to displace
dumplings fretting among the bubbles,
cinnamon attendant, swirl and steam.

Happily it's not empty even yet.
Many feasts and many toasts gone by,
it nurtures a scatter of minty plants.
Crowding from its innards, they crane
to see what we will see in them.

How quiet they keep
about their heart-
shaped leaves.

BRYAN PODMORE

Summer Storm

The heavy clothes of the heat
weighed her down, day and night.
She could not recall so long a drought.
No breath troubled the wheat, no tremble
invaded the calm of oak leaves.
Every long, still day there was no relief.

All that August she slept fitfully, hot palms
oiling her brow, till she dreamt,
one midnight, of wild horses on the loose.
Through the centre of her sleep
they ran, a dozen black stallions, their
animal engines pumping steam and sweat.

They shook the peace from the sea.
On barn and hill they drummed.
They stormed the pasture and took
the lane, then, as her breath matched theirs,
they beat on all her walls at once.
She knew the shine on their flanks,
saw the ripple of merciless muscle
and cried to see how their nostrils flared.
Then suddenly she woke, among
a tangle of white sheets, afraid.

Rain was falling into the trees.
The dawn grew. The sky had broken
at last. She went outside, felt bare soles
gladden to the touch of wet earth.
From apple tree boughs large drops
cooled her nakedness. A bird began,
and, far westward, she thought she sensed
the gallop of horses riding the clouds.
She could almost hear them. She stood,
fingers easing through damp hair,
and listened, straining for a hoofbeat.

CHRISTOPHER ALLAN

Staples

I was meant to guard the unlockable bus
but got held up at the stone circle
when the hill ponies came to worship.
I wandered away but a young chestnut
befriended me and led me back
into the circle, where she grazed quietly
as long as I sat on a stone.
Out of the bracken came a powerful grey pony
who broke my heart because she so reminded me of Misty.
The others stopped grazing and turned to stare.
She was aloof and wouldn't be touched
but led me to the second largest stone
the Mother stone?
where she stood in communion for an age
occasionally touching her soft muzzle
against the ancient hardness.
A succession of ponies joined her,
stayed a moment, touched the stone, moved away.
I may have been brought here for a purpose
so I try to make my peace with the past.

We bring you grain from the far plain.
We bring you flower garlands from the hedgetops.
We bring the first milk to pour at your centre.
We sit back to back while the maidens wrap
plaited ivy around each stone, link
and trail them back to the centre.
We rock and hum and by turns dance our slow dance.
We shriek out our darkest fears of the deep night
that the stars do not fall from the sky
and burn the land as they did in our forefathers' time.
That the great white dust does not come back
and kill the beasts in the fields
and the smallest ones at the fireside.
We keep the boys beyond the outer ring of fires.
The stave men do not let them to the centre
till they have whooped and raged
and the wild is danced out of them.

MIRANDA TITE

Photograph of the Year

Reading clockwise from left to right:
Johnny Leeper, Gill, Ed Knowles, my father,
each, like a stylite, on his crop of Cornish rock.
Wearing knee-length hiking-shorts and boots,
and showing the five-day shadow of a beard,
they stare through the eye of the storm
and a sixty-foot-high column of spume.
Did they hear the furious Prussian music
that would leap up at them over the waves,
like Brunnhilde, and jigger their lives? Did they
wonder where the seabirds had flown? Birds,
if they had known, that would have pecked out their eyes
and dropped them on the beach like precious shells
for beadsmen and women to count in their retreats.

MICHAEL HENRY

All Souls

Under the table
the musician lies on his back,
setting the pitch,
playing the long, sad notes.

Then he sings:
about a faraway flute,
the taste of a distance
where plums drop on to the lawn.

He sings about the stop
in the tunnel, moments
before the station, of
someone who almost arrived.

It is for this that he sings:
swan, neck stretched out from Siberia,
led by stars or ultrasonic murmurs,
the one that never flies in.

He sings for all those who are
slime, sperm, clot, left behind
in the gap, who missed the way
into life.

In E major, *con brio*,
he sings of arriving, settling,
light coming on in a window,
closing; about the way of it.

He loses the pitch,
tongue-tied: listens
as they gather round
the kitchen table.

BRENDA LEALMAN

Distance over Speed

We are growing large and old
without imagination—
if only we could reinterpret
the distance between sounds
and silence.

Between the cry and tender touch

Time is the distance over speed.
Swifts have no sense of it,
leaning on counter-rotating clouds
that draw a moveable membrane
over moon and stars.

Between music's end and memories beginning

Far below, close to the hub,
whales hear the *basso profundo*
of their slower world, note the rising tenor
of a passing wave, the stiletto of a storm
and the undulate wind.

Between speech and the wait for a reply

Time in its old familial casings
has workings for now profitless.
All is instinct. Our human artifice exists
without its old inherent way of knowing
when we are to come, to stay, to go.

Between the dog's sharp bark and the turning key

Let me tell you a story then
about a man who once conceived
the perfect simile for life:
a thorny, cobalt-coloured rose that budded,
bloomed, was blown in but one day.

How long have you got?

TRICIA TORRINGTON

Moonshadow

*Total eclipse of the sun
seen from the Somme battlefield, 11. 8. 99.*

Moonshadow out on a rally drive
—sun going off like a gun at my back,
racing at 2000 miles an hour,

Nova Scotia to the Bay of Bengal:
over Headland Point, up Ticklemore Street,
chasing along the Longueval road.

Sun, I'm a trick ahead of you,
knowing my slot,
the way I fit exactly today

over your furnace
ninety three million miles
away behind me.

My moon face is metalled, black,
rock solid. Usually you think of me
like lichen or a crochet jug cover.

Delville Wood,
and brambles, stumps, rusted wire
hold me back.

I rummage in the shadowy bottom,
turn on a sour green light,
a night light in an aquarium.

X-ray figures come out,
slide along Devil's Trench,
into Rotten Row, King Street,

Strand. So many things
are seen in my dark:
I'm like a boot heel crushing.

I put a stop to birdsong,
leave a skyline of fire.
I dare what is tar-skinned

to undo its padlock, come out.
Shell sounds, a boney cry:
that was Captain Benton,

he was left behind,
alive, without his legs.
Because of my screen

you're better seen today, sun;
I show up the churn and sprout
around your boiling edge.

I use you, too:
your nuclear reactor helps me
on my way down Caterpillar Valley.

Sun, you're slipping from me,
becoming a pinprick of light
in a piece of card.

I know now: you're nothing more
than a lump of gas, a star,
a G_2V yellow dwarf.

BRENDA LEALMAN

The Earth is Thirsty

on this earth which is thirsty and takes them back into itself again
(Rolf Jacobsen: 'The age of the great symphonies')

Go find my father
slumped behind the door
his dead finger
on a dictionary
pointing to a word
that sent him straight
to heaven.

Unearth his burly arms
and fingers lacing
spires of scarlet flowers
along a spine of beansticks.

Call out my name in a dream
and you may find me
burrowing in the uncomprehending
dark at his feet
smudging purple through
a blue cabbage patch
tapping petals onto sap-green
stems
pegging gold through ragged grasses
into gleaming compost to fire
a vermilion fence.

Tone on tone with crayons hard as bone
those hours melted on the page
form & shadow were my rage
and I was blind to everything
but the drawing

while he leaned on his fork tines
smiling a rakish smile
the wheelbarrow upturned like a mythic
bell, its underside clinging to
darkened seedheads.

I was immured from knowing
what roots were pulling me down
pouring out new shoots of colour
through my hand, impatient to find

the stronghold in the earth
this row of cabbage plants had found.

Then what was planted in me
in my blood
like seeds underground
was a hood of air
wrapped round a rainbow

so that when I rose
from the drawing
line & colour
still pouring out of me

I was moonwalking, an alien
crossing stepping-stones of the soul
over our garden

re-entering the cave-dark kitchen

the vision of my parents
propped up talking
distant as the moon

while a word imploded
swift as a comet

paradiso:

his finger pressing
to his lips
like a secret
overbrimming

as I stood there
clutching my sketchbook

Unnursed . . . unbred . . .
blown clean through . . .

RITA CARTER

James K. Baxter
1926–1972

James K. Baxter is a New Zealand poet who achieved an international reputation in the days when Oxford had an international poetry list. I was lucky enough to be reviewing for Alan Ross, who had an international outlook anyway, and he handed me Baxter's posthumous collection, *Runes* (1973). Conscientious reviewer that I was, I found a copy of Baxter's first Selected Poems, *The Rock Woman* (1969), on the shelves in Blackwell's and read my way into the work of a poet who was to become a touchstone for me.

I knew nothing then of Baxter's final phase, of his immersion in the counter-culture—the underground, as we called it—from which I had just emerged. What fascinated me was his fusion of the imaginative and the everyday, the way he could drive down on to Waipatiki Beach 'By a bad road, banging in second gear' and enter a landscape that belongs to

> the oldest Venus,
> Too early for the books, ubiquitous,
>
> The manifold mother to whom my poems go
> Like ladders down—

Better than any modern poet I know, Baxter can recreate the medieval sense of this earth as middle earth, with other dimensions above and below.

He was born into a radical family—his father was a conscientious objector in the First World War who was taken all the way to the Western Front and tied to a pole—and began his own rebellion early, drinking himself into a Rimbaudesque disordering of all the senses. He became a Catholic convert, one of the very few who can make religious feeling accessible to the sceptic, and ended living out a dream in which a voice told him to go to Jerusalem. He found a Maori village of that name where he lived as a barefoot Franciscan figure, running a commune for drop-outs and drug victims. His poems from that period are wonderful, moving from a wry, self-mocking humour to moments of faith when he can shrug off his doubts and bodily ills, which were real enough. He died of a heart attack at forty-six. He was given a Maori funeral and young people from all over New Zealand trekked to get there.

Extraordinary as his life was, it was all of a piece. His last days bore out the qualities I found in the poems I first read, the poems of a troubled family man, trying to marry his responsibilities to the demands of the imagination. Poetry for Baxter was never a literary exercise. It was always for real. I wrote my Homage to him in 1975 and, at the risk of showing my older self up, I am reprinting it here because the poem that gave me my starting point, 'Letter from the Mountains', seems to have struck a chord with other members of the group. Indeed, David Hart has taken as epigraph for his poem the very same lines that I took as epigraph for mine:

> Despair is the only gift;
> When it is shared, it becomes a different thing ...

ROGER GARFITT

Letter from the Mountains

There was a message. I have forgotten it.
There was a journey to make. It did not come to anything.
But these nights, my friend, under the iron roof
Of this old rabbiters' hut where the traps
Are still hanging up on nails,
Lying in a dry bunk, I feel strangely at ease.
The true dreams, those longed-for strangers,
Begin to come to me through the gates of horn.

I will not explain them. But the city, all that other life
In which we crept sadly like animals
Through thickets of dark thorns, haunted by the moisture of women
And the rock of barren friendship, has now another shape.
Yes, I thank you. I saw you rise like a Triton,
A great reddish gourd of flesh,
From the sofa at that last party, while your mistress smiled
That perfect smile, and shout as if drowning—
'You are always—'
> Despair is the only gift;
When it is shared, it becomes a different thing; like rock, like water;
And so you also can share this emptiness with me.

Tears from faces of stone. They are our own tears.
Even if I had forgotten them
The mountain that has taken my being to itself
Would still hang over this hut, with the dead and the living
Twined in its crevasses. My door has forgotten how to shut.

JAMES K. BAXTER

from *Runes* (1973) reproduced by permission of Oxford University Press Australia from *Collected Poems: James K. Baxter*, John Weir (ed.), OUP, 1995 © Oxford University Press

Homage to James K. Baxter

A newsagent taking in the first papers
would see us taking shape at the counter,
the ghost trade, come for Mars and Old Holborn, sugar and smoke.

Each morning, a shortchanging of the shadows,
as they rose from areas and stairwells,
sleepless from skinpopping methedrine.

Ah! the nights on the road
on a mattress, 'on the move' through
the bleak indoors. Joe Tex sang of

stogies as we rolled our Social Security
into straights, played '*Indianapoly*' through the small hours:
the speed kings, firing on half an amp.

And yet it was almost good, to be one
of a tacit company, to be men without women,
low lifeforms in a basement room.

Only a few of us became serious ghosts.
Our selves shadowed us. Only the present
can be lost in Lethe,

as I would lose it now, for your company.
But the light breaks. And already the shapes
are forming at the counter.

ROGER GARFITT

Letter from the Mountain

Living way up here
what can I tell you?
That I am glad
to be above your struggles,
that my bones are still
unfrozen, and that my flesh
continues to hang together
about its spiky rod?

Built to box out trouble
this cabin on a rock's lip
has been a haven for me
but a strange journey began
inwards when I woke
one rain-lashed dawn.

Having no-one here to sound off
it was not long before the whisky
made a firm friend, and my soup pan
warming on the stove became a presence.
I'm rapidly losing it under this sky
of terrible planets. The omens are bad.
I've begun talking to candles.

This is my last letter to you.
Please pass it around but draw
no definite conclusions.
My signature's an empty circle
sounding with rumours.
Can you hear the hard weather?

CHRISTOPHER ALLAN

Despair

I need you, fellow poets,
scramblers after the right words,
turning up, bringing a packed lunch.

The right words for what?
I need another cup of tea,
another walk.

In the rollcall for the gift of despair
silence is speech.

Out of it, the memory,
the poem.

Little boy who runs along beside me,
wide-eyed, in tears almost, chuckling,
skipping and hopping, his little heart heaving,
a sigh escaping him almost
huger than the big bang.

Come along, come along.

DAVID HART

The Other Company

Once in a month of Sundays
it draws up:

not the familiar bus,
built of misgivings,

whose engine labours
under a rattle of flaps,

whose exhaust is a spew
of midnight oil,

but the well-tempered bus
riveted with light,

the bus that pulls in
out of nowhere,

with just one seat left
on the long bench.

ROGER GARFITT

Dream Warden

It's hot and we are waiting for them to bring the canoes.
Sixteen yr old Tom has taken off his shirt and is
leaning back on one golden arm like a young
                                                    Adonis
sitting on the blue-grey boards of the landing stage
staring at water, then back at his cousin, one as fair
as the other dark, perspectives shift under their
gaze. They know what they are doing now but not who
                                                    they are yet . . .

It's Northern Michigan, deep in Indian country. They
are getting into it now, having clambered over rocky
boulders, slivered through waterfalls, narrow gorges
and miniature rapids. My brother-in-law leads one
canoe with my youngest in the middle and me taking
                                                    the stern.

He paddles left and I right. We are a good team, unlike
my sister-in-law and my husband who are arguing. Too
many chiefs and not enough Indians, thinks my nine yr old son,
who grips the sides like a young brave, his dark fringe
flying up in a feather headdress as the canoe circles
and dives into the bank. The bar at my feet braced

taut as a crossbow, my back feels sun patches,

soft ponderances of warmth sliding over each other
like pebbles in my pocket—

the current rocks us onwards, clear water accelerating
the pull of my paddle shovelling bubbles.

Turning a bend, I notice silhouettes, fluid, shimmering
in the heat haze, high up on the bank. Smoke drifts from
tepees as they watch me watching them, paddle raised till they
pass out of sight. I look back for the rest of the tribe
but they are not visible, just the river racing on, all
                                                    glitter
and skim. It could carry us off any place. Arrowheads of
                                                    light
break through foliage above, cradling us in dark leaf
                                                    shadows
spilling over our bodies, rephrasing the water's surface.
I obey water that sweeps everything away with it, rainbows
trees, stones, holds only the silence hidden in its shadows.

High up in the unending blue little gold cloud puffs dwindle
like smoke signals, the sun scouting the way.

My daughter's sunburned shoulder blades are apache-brown
                                      beneath blue U-shaped
dungarees knotted in a bow just below the middle of her back.
Her chestnut bangs flow down and swell over her shoulder's
                                                rim
like brown tributaries of the river and her motionless arms
are soft as the backs of plump fish.

As the water snakes and glides in an unbroken chute and wave,
I hear the shouts and chortles of cousins splashing,
playfighting, breaking off branches

to thrash each other with leaves.

My brother-in-law doesn't turn. His back is small and neat in
                                            his check shirt.
Single-minded, he does not let his thoughts stray to left
or right of him. Experience heals quickly on his skin like
water in this heat. For him the river is not a riddle,

he's a middle-of-the-road man, ignoring the waterfall's slow weep,
passing chimeras, the current pushing what is beyond forever
away from him.

For me the river is a long dream letting go its beauty
slowly from our wake. I burn in the present, watching the
                                                  prow
uncoiling silver water. Later there will be turbulence,
                                                loss,
a constriction beneath the weight, then slow deliverance
as silence surfaces—

but for now I am possessed by the river: Dream Warden
                                                    protector
from dark dreams.

RITA CARTER

Conversion

Again they have me back on the bed—
my Promethean rock, my criminal's cross—
three years of uselessness, well-meant intentions
never thought through; yet more by rejection—

all that passion, dedication, belief
in each other, the pain and reward
of our children, frightened away forever
by the challenge to which he could not rise—

thieves of the good life, we had no need
of philosophy. And all of a sudden condemned
to trolleys, slammed doors, routines that others
choose and impose, the hyssop and vinegar

of my hourly ventilator: all landmarks gone,
I pined for some new world of certainty,
some affirmation of shared understanding,
a love that would not shrink away.

A newcomer still, this morning I shared
once more in the Host, while the sanctified blood
and the image of Mary and her Child
in their sad haunting resonance confirmed

a partial rebirth in which, here on the bed,
sheet wrinkles straightened, pillows arranged,
food plates and cups on their usual tray
now removed, I can again read, and pray.

JOHN HARRISON

Missing

*The Thiepval Memorial on the Somme
commemorates 'The Missing'*

I heard the sky
over Thiepval.
It was full
of metal and fire.

I must not remember
the sky over Gloucestershire,
the shimmer, furred flare of bluebells.

Siftings of you are all around.
I'll put you in my handbag,
try piecing the fragments together.

The bits I'm leaving behind
will hop and stutter.
A rusty custard tin

is working its way
from under ground
near to where you fell.

You're making echoes in there,
in that giant emptiness. A curved
stone bench waits for the Missing.

There was one
George Nugent, came back
eighty four years later.

In the first blue flare
when I put the gas fire on,
I listen for your return.

The card with your
four last words
turns into the silk
of your skin.

BRENDA LEALMAN

Don Engine

The sun sounds like this.
I heard it once:
hiss, distant thrum,
clatter in the sky.

I hear it now in Sheffield:
Don Engine gingered, nags,
begins to pedal pistons, ten tons
of wet steam on each.

12,000 horsepower giant
judders, pounds on earth,
thumps out steel currents,
imperial gunboats in armour plate.

Pause: the giant growls
at those who detest their work,
makes a flaring sky,
an upward chasm.

And below, land crumbles
to a *sceath*:
sceath field, Sheffield,
border along open land;

edge where junked metal breaks,
burns to rust in acid soil,
becomes shocked waves,
zillions of protons, vapours.

Where it is broken,
out of crud by the stiff river,
a fig tree, *ficus carica*,
bears fruit soft as chiffon.

BRENDA LEALMAN

Gathered In

(Llandrindod Old Church 2000)

Around this rough ground, the wind-raked grasses,
the peat pools and sphagnum hollows,
a few families had a sort of life,
Swydd Neithion and this small church
holding all they had in common.
Springs gave waters the cattle wouldn't touch,
thin soil on the slopes yielding
all they knew of bread and ale.

This church was the soul's byre.
They trod-in their faith with the mud from their feet,
their Welsh voices calling the angels in
like errant cattle.

Three lords of the manor, shareholders all,
knowing these waters and another worth,
brought the railway and enclosure act,
pegging neat angles on the wet ground
for hotel, spa and concert hall,
the tea room and the tennis court.
In this little Harrogate in Radnorshire
a frock-coat-and-bustle parish church
was the least the patrons could expect,
the new nave's darker spaces—far back from the crystal angels—
enfolding chambermaids, grooms and boot boys.

On the eastern slopes above the new town
the old church holds them still,
the shepherds and the waitresses, postmen and farriers.

In the graveyard they have this in common:

rain on an angel's wing.

GAVIN HOOSON

dom sylvester houedard
1924–1992

He seems history already but not long ago he was very much alive, writing his name all lower case or typically signing his work simply 'dsh'. He was not a foreign writer—he was born in the Channel Islands—but has been allowed into this series as from an edge of language. Perhaps from the far reaches of the exploration of consciousness.

Dom Sylvester was a Benedictine monk who seemed to be given considerable freedom to follow his instincts and facility for dialogue with monks and others of other faiths, as well as to engage with other poets. He was a natural link with Buddhism and I found later writings by him on the Muslim mystic in the journal of the eponymous Ibn 'Arabi Society. And within the Christian traditions he wrote on Meister Eckhart among others and within the Catholic tradition he had been one of the team who had translated the Jerusalem Bible. One time when I saw him he gave me a copy of a piece he'd just published on Samuel Beckett. I'm sure there was much more he was and did that I didn't know about and am surprised there has been no biography or collected writings.

And I'm sure his more traditional poetry and concrete poetry and drawings (and how inadequate any of these categories seem for what he did) cannot properly be encountered without some sense of his whole adventuring life. He seemed to me dour *and* fun, a passionate *and* a calm man. His version of the Basho frog-pond haiku has a wonderful simplicity and delight to it:

> frog
> pond
> plop

It's all there, isn't it, and more? I think it was this elusive *and more* that attracted me to him and his work. You will know what I mean when I say I felt he was *on to something*.

Of course, his 'whole adventuring life', as I've described it, was mostly as a Christian monk but I rather think it was as one who worked essentially across boundaries to such an extent that his awareness was of *our being* and of the *one Being* and of a dissolving of the one in the other. While he was utterly rigorous in what he did—one might say, utterly rigorously playful—he was as far from being a dogmatist or apologist for a single point of view as ever I've met.

In the workshop we wondered about how his 'work' (did he call it *work*? I'm not sure) developed and why. About his *voice*, whether he wrote at all for speaking—he was obviously a typewriter freak. And I suggested a technique he used himself from the *I Ching*, tossing two coins to make hexagrams (an unbroken line if they came down on the same side, a broken line if they didn't) and working from the patterns.

I don't find myself imitating Dom Sylvester, as I have done other poets, but I do have a hunch—or different hunches at different times—that he opened or pointed to ways I'd like to travel; or along asides from them.

DAVID HART

22   starting to catch
            in hollows of the hills
          the yielding
      dark & just
           gives form to the firm
         clear & still
     the form of heaven
       is the form of the people

       contemplate it in the above
        & discover change
      contemplate it in the people
       & change the world

            the situation
     means fire without a plan
wont beautify the heights

               while things stay controversial
     let the white horse flap its wings
       to
          woo the right time
      for the 4th
with 9 so far off at the top
    & 6 so weak in the 2nd
          to decide
       on either outer brilliance
      or inner conviction

     with dark & just as form
       love and light as content CLINGS

30

[One section from the sequence of poems based on a cycle of 12 hexagrams of the *I Ching*, the 2nd draft dated in his dating 770808.] Reproduced by kind permission of Prinknash Abbey. The dsh archive is in the keeping of the John Rylands Library in Manchester.

The Tao of the Keys

The typewriter speaks
& Dom Sylvester is lost again

Words fall out of nowhere
smirch the silence on the paper
are shaken into   a birth

The starting point is simple
        a cradle rocks

Warm skin   a breast   a blanket
        a great cry

Into time the timeless enters

Again words dream
The tap of keys after Compline
        the candle low

& language becomes a bridge
        the strange syntax
bearing the soul's weight

long or little the span reaches
        new ground
a change in perspective opens

        a phase of insanity?

Yet still the typewriter speaks
& Dom Sylvester is on to something

It is better to name God
with a verb than a noun

How the silence is covered
with the snow-tracks of birds
        page after page

But something more than half wise
        less than half mad
has flown away
or maybe catches its breath
        unheeded under the white

CHRISTOPHER ALLAN

Three hexagram poems

You hold
back,
don't you?
You hold
back,
don't you?

When you feel the river is cloudy, and there is no firm bottom,
you thrash about, seeking for a foothold.

Keeping
still
still
still
is hard
to learn

If the fountain were flowing,
how could I watch it begin to flow?

Water flows
clear
above
steadily
settling
sediment

If the gate were not closed,
how could I open it?

CHARLES JOHNSON

Broken Lines

These hexagrams
say no

more than yes
say flow

more than stay
yet leave me

married neither
to the first

nor the last:
but a pull

pressures me
for the *less*

to be *more*
as though

I am
a tethered boat

keel to flood
and God

is wondering
whether He'll

let slip
the rope

that anchors
me fast

CHRISTOPHER ALLAN

Hexagrams at Walcot

1.
Evens,   some flow,
         some boxed in-ness.

Windows open,
         windows closed.

 If the woodpecker knows,
 she is going about her peckingness
 without saying.

                  Tree house in the wood
         well rooted
                  available to storm.
   Mud
         is solid earth,
                  is so wet I can slip easily.

2.
Who is trying to put a roof on my chest?

         To trap me safely in.

   Such ambiguity about my freedom
to flame and smoke and perspire and evaporate

or to let the flame curl down
         and the smoke be blown away
         and the sweat dry out
         and the blood cool
                  down the plughole

         ready as it is.

3.
Someone
is on the roof
watching the river.

I am that someone
on the roof
watching the river.

I see now several rivers
passing under the building
asking what the building is
and why
wondering how strong it is.
and why.

If the building collapses
how far is there to fall
and into whose arms?

DAVID HART

Cover

On a country road between oaks and limes
among cattle and pigeons, easy to miss
in broken tarmac, water and mud,
an iron rectangle surprises,
an iron card as if thrown at random:
forty one diamonds around the words
FIRE HYDRANT, which someone, somewhere,
once cast in a furnace of poisoned air;
evidence of a man-made underworld,
some engineered Lethe not understood
because unseen. Such labour long ago
but to what purpose? What was the fear?

JOHN HARRISON

Waiting

Walking back from the farm
I pause where the tarmac gives way to green track,
where the small stream curves towards summer
and gathers whatever is white to it.

Evening, and I've come here to wait
by this cool, wet stone at the foot of the bridge—
wait to see how the sky lifts the light
from the water and how the hills come closer . . .

how the haze that smudges the toothaching sound
of the forage harvester suddenly loosens and
spreads, increasing the space around,
how escaping green rushes the horizon;

for the moment that always isn't quite
finally to arrive, inching through the leaves
and the dark of the water under the site
of the bowed alder to open inside me.

CAROLINE GOURLAY

Between Two Worlds

Dolley Old Bridge
Llanfair Hill
Pen Offa
Lower Spoad
Cwmsanahan Hill

Ditchyeld Bridge
Llan y Felin
Herrock Cottage
Broken Bank

Panpunton
Gilfach yr Heol
Garbett Hall
Bwlch

JOHN HARRISON

God the Passenger

So God is a verb, not a noun,
always on the move, *necessarily present
in all predications*. Will you find God
running for the train and will he just miss it

like us mortals, or split himself in two,
one part flying in through an open carriage window
while the other, briefcase-waving half
stamps about the platform, hurling insults?

And as God is a verb, not a noun,
he'll not sit still on the train
but pace up and down so the doors
hush open and shut, open and shut,

and annoy the other passengers
while God makes a scene on the platform...
But *necessarily present* means God can't hang around
so platform God speaks to train God

on the mobile and there's a great (late) coming together
at Platform Nine . . . *We apologise for the late running
of this God* . . . and God greets God
like a longlost sibling, or a child found.

AMANDA ATTFIELD

Nut Case

Robbed, this chestnut case, split
like a gutted hedgehog,
its insides open, robbed.

Curled in its soft corner,
what's left? A brown sliver,
quite unappetising.

Squirrel or mouse had thought
to leave a logo, shaped,
spread like a maple leaf,

a stain to testify
to imperfection's ease,
to chide my shot at polish

as the prickles assault
my prying hands. *Keep out
your dodgy words!* they say.

BRYAN PODMORE

tear along dotted line
— — — — — — — — — — — — — — — — — —

Whole line
Broken Line
Whole Line
Broken Line
Broken Line
Whole Line

Hexagram

Bar code

This poem is past its sell-by date
and should be removed forthwith

RICHARD BEAUMOND

Juan Ramón Jiménez
1888–1958

Jimenez was one of the founders of the modern movement in Spanish poetry and an important influence on later poets such as Lorca. To readers outside Spain he is probably best known for his long prose-poem, *Platero and I*, an evocation of his donkey, Platero, which must be the most unlikely of masterpieces, so full of lyric invention that it transcends any suspicion of sentimentality.

As a young man Jimenez had been a good painter and, though he stopped painting once he became absorbed in poetry, his sensitivity to the qualities of light is apparent in the poem I have translated here.

TRICIA TORRINGTON

Winter Scene: Snow

    Where have the colours hidden away
on this black and white day?
The flora, black; the water, grey; the sky
and the land, of a pallid chiaroscuro;
and the city dejected
as an old etching by a romantic.

    The lonely figure walking, black;
black the bird, startled,
that hisses like an arrow across the garden . . .
Even the silence is unpainted and hardens.

The dusk falls. The heavens
have not even a sweetness. The sundown
has a vague yellowyness, that is nearly brilliant,
that is nearly not so. Beyond this, the countryside
is all dry iron.
    And enter the night,
funereal; in mourning
and totally cold, without even stars, white
and black, like the day, black and white.

Juan Ramón Jiménez: from *Poemas májicos y dolientes* (1909) translated by Tricia Torrington and Carlos Alvarez

Poem

Not only to see
the bush
but to feel the spring wind
as its thumbs comb
a panic of leaves

Not only to see
the ocean
but to hear its rollers fall
& follow the *thuck* & sway
teasing wrack & stone

Not only to see
the clouds come
but to witness their slow weighting
(grey swans with black bellies)
& then the rain

Not only to see
but to seek the lines
waiting to be shaped from these
as squall & spume & leaf
borrow your voice to speak

CHRISTOPHER ALLAN

Snow on Our Hill

A seasonal dressing softly appeared
today on our hill. We climbed to relish
the remembered crunch, to find the same garnish
on all the hills far into distance, laid
with precisely the same level baseline
and each one at the same modest height,
a broken but clear-cut horizon of white
as though carefully drawn by some craftsman
under strict orders. A moving effect:
enough for still air with so little rise
to be colder, as we know it goes on
always colder and thinner to summits
of mountains, to airline trails and beyond.
How fine is the film that holds all our lives.

JOHN HARRISON

Aura

Dejad las puertas abiertas
esta noche, por si él
quiere, esta noche, venir,
que está muerto
      Jiménez

I keep the small door open for the dead
to come in
      from their penumbra
of silence, sadness, though they carry
black weights of immense indifference
to come in
      by pushing at my border
as if it were water

To wait in stillness for an inner eye
to open
      like a white flower from a green bud
to look beyond things for that trick of light
for something greater than its sum
to open myself
      and see past the border
as if I saw through water

To lie at eye-level with skin
is to focus
      on a prism of oil
with its pale universe of glistening stars,
electricity; to see the silvered moon
is to focus
      on the exact same imagery
as if looking through water

To keep the door open is for the dead
to enter
      to see past one reality
to let the risk of darkness descending
take over, see past it to another kind of light
to enter
      the world of the soul
reflected on the skin of all dark water

TRICIA TORRINGTON

So I set off

(With Jiménez at Walcot Hall, January 2000)

So I set off with my friend Jim,
solitary, both of us, but needing company,
and after some conversation about scanning
we fall silent and go each our own way.

I happen now across Betty, who asks me,
'What are words for really?'
and I say, 'To answer that
I need to go out in a small boat.'

But I don't do it.
From the harbour wall
I watch a small boat far out
off balance turn into its own wake.

All day and into the night I watch the small boat far out
chasing its tail
until the moon seems right
and the boat lets out something like a screech
and lurches violently away
to an island I have heard
was once inhabited.

Walking back lonely from the sea
I can't look Betty in the eye.

My friend Jim is at the gate waiting for me.
He says, 'Darkness is so careless,
it leaves its poems lying everywhere
for anyone to see nakedly.'

And down the lane still Betty
waits for an answer. I say to myself, 'One day I shall go
far out in a small boat, one day I shall look Betty
in the eye.'

DAVID HART

Awareness of White

And you come down to this, one morning,
a morning of small bird song.
When the sea is calm,
its bed rippled from a gentle sleep,
when even seagulls daytrip somewhere else . . .
while the tide is turning
how it does,
with the small breaths of one still asleep,
or half asleep, and the daylight, too,
only half awake, muted.

You come down to an awareness of salt
while by the shore the water is waiting.

Then, later, as different, as sudden as temper,
challenged by the wind, stirred up by clouds racing . . .
maybe it is evening, or later in the year,
you come down to this...
the beach gorse flattened to green streaks
on burnt ochre, and umberish stones,
and those stones piled in drifts, in terraces and ditches,
while the tide turns out with deep breaths,
with a haunting, and real bluster.

An awareness of white,
in unlimited shades.

TRICIA TORRINGTON

Mists

Your cleaned boots wait in a cupboard
while you are trapped here,
all you really need in easy reach.
Your eyes search the pale walls for comfort.

A large sheep stares at you from sedge, challenging.
The rest of the flock go away down Ogwen valley.
Beyond a wire fence sparse pasture is strewn with slate.
A few faint telegraph poles cross the view, going nowhere.
That strange mound must conceal a place of sanctuary,
a shepherd's or an ancient hermit's hut.

A band of thin blue light parts the swelling slopes

to hint at a place you mislaid one distant sultry dawn
and must get back to.
The mountain wears a hoop of broken white.
White highlights five serrated peaks
as though undercoat is drying several colours.

The distant valley steams enticingly.
At the edge of vision lies another mountain range
your boots are itching to explore.

Next month is a pale horse in a golden meadow.

MIRANDA TITE

A Chance of the Light

The shadow of a hedge,
feather-perfect on the snow:

the brushwork in even bars,
as if pressed from the side
of the brush, and pressing out

a summer dust, a lilac shadow
I slide over the brown
of your shoulder, lift away

from the freckle on your breast.

ROGER GARFITT

The Blooming of the Gorse

a wedding toast

Now is the miraculous pairing of stag and hen:
all theatrical props and screens folded away,
Act V Scene V in a Shakespearean play
when lovers plot their line of best fit through the stars.
The game of Conceal and Reveal is over
as we watch bride and groom cut into the cake
and there's breath on the blade of the knife.

Now that I'm a kind of twelfth man to the proceedings,
I'm reminded of my twelfth birthday cake, baked
by the cake-maker to the Grand Duke of Luxembourg:
a sponge cricket square with stumps,
white chocolate fielders and a cherry ball.
It brings back long, hot, sunshiny summers,
season after season, boundary after boundary,
and partnerships that go on and on forever.

Today it is nearly Spring.
Gorse describes the landscape on the hills.
Soon it will burst into flower.
As bride and groom kiss
I'm reminded of the old saying and raise my glass
to kissing, back in fashion before the blooming of the gorse.

MICHAEL HENRY

Eugenio Montale
1896–1981

Jonathan Galassi, the American poet whose sensitive translations have made Montale accessible as never before, writes of his 'nervous, astringent music'. He shuttles between a sense of the material weight of existence, the sheer drag of it, and a sense of its lightness, the way it can dissolve at any moment. This can be seen most vividly in his sequence, *Mediterranean*, which draws on the rough coast of the Cinque Terre he had known from childhood. *Mediterranean* is truly modern in a way few poems are, catching the flicker of a consciousness evolved out of the materials of the universe and trying to make sense of it.

ROGER GARFITT

>I stand amid the rubble
>that scales down to you, down
>to the steep bank above you,
>prone to landslides, yellow, etched
>by rivers of rainwater.
>My life is this dry slope,
>a means not an end, a way
>open to runoff from gutters and slow erosion.
>And it's this, too: this plant
>born out of devastation
>that takes the sea's lashing in the face,
>hanging in the wind's erratic gales.
>This piece of grassless earth
>broke open so a daisy could be born.
>In her I nod towards the sea that offends me,
>silence is still missing from my life.
>I watch the glistening earth,
>the air so blue it goes dark.
>And what rises in me, sea,
>may be the rancour
>that each son feels for his father.
>
>EUGENIO MONTALE: from *Mediterraneo* (1924) translated by Jonathan Galassi and reprinted by kind permission of Farrar, Straus & Giroux LLC and Carcanet Press.

Don't bark at me

(Aberystwyth, 1950s; Shropshire, February 2000)

Don't bark at me, cat,
it can't be as strange as that,
the givenness. The fishing boats that went out in the bay
        brought back no oranges,
        and I never heard anyone say the sea had no right
        to fly up over the promenade
        and break down walls
        and flood the streets.

    Nasal sprays
     were not used for knees, pessaries
               were not used for eyes, poultices
                           were not made to be eaten.

    In my father's laboratory I learned to pipette urine samples
    and to read the signs, I learned
    that we have different bloods
    and they need matching.

Don't bite me, snowdrops,
it can't be as strange as that,
the givenness. The sun that went down over the bay
        didn't burn the sky away.

    Analgesics
        were not for watering the flowers, emetics
                were not for picnics, expectorants
                          were not given out in church.

    In my father's laboratory I learned the work of white coats,
    that ice cream could carry typhoid,
    and what guinea pigs were used for.

Don't trip me up, grass,
contingency
can't be like that for us. The battleship that anchored in the bay
        had not been merely playing at war
        but all I smelt then on its deck
        was the clean salty metal.

You won't mourn me, cedars,
contingency
won't shed those tears. Poetry was
> *the curfew tolls the knell of parting day*
> and Welsh was the language of the angels,
> puritanical ones, upright, orderly.

> Potatoes
> > were not handed out for the school photo, broken biscuits
> > > were not given out in assembly, crates of milk
> > > > didn't come from cormorants.

From my father's on-call work I learned of the boy
broken by the bus,
pulled out dying from underneath it
by his father crying.

> This was order,
> these were the rules.

DAVID HART

Cracks

A river system pictured from space;
veins on the back of your hand:
the cracks on the ceiling
had their own life drawn against white
& held their own story
(but it was our story too).

My father said they were Hitler's work:
stray bombs meant for Liverpool
veering to us in the suburbs.
Bebington was victim: windows broke
chimneys fell & the buried bones
around St Andrew's shook.

The room could be multiplied
in the dressing-table mirror.
Side mirrors reflected your face,
multi-angled, down a corridor of light.
Any flaw could be seen
repeated & repeated in the glass.

I sat there silent,
glad to have missed the raids,
but my eyes could see how evil
still tracks to our time:
a strange light running through mirrors
& that tremor-trace above.

Once I tried to think up a world
without cracks, perfect as crystal.
I must have known that cracks ran
throughout that house & any possible house
& were widening under our feet
as we grew & flourished.

It was easier to imagine the night
of shaken walls: flares & flak
bombers like regimented bees
the earth taking blow after blow
& somewhere above the fire-struck sky
Venus & Mars never further apart.

CHRISTOPHER ALLAN

A Building of Rooks

At the juice bar I order orange pressé,
note the pith that would not pass through a strainer.

In the same way memories of my mother
squeezing oranges for us, the warhead
of the squeezer gored with fruit, sometimes
blood orange trickling into a glass moat
with a tiny notch for her to pour from.

As we grew older, she would wait on us:
squash with a high density of Vitamin C,
while we played out our boyhoods on the starched
shirtfront pitches of eternal summer.
In the quiet lighting of late afternoon,

when cricket stumps looked like old men's alopecia legs,
while we were waiting for a final bat
we would play Mephistopheles to her Faust,
trying to tempt her Fifties innocence
with cigarettes and smutty schoolboy stories.

Yes, there were whitecoated men,
and floating across the fields
black birds, like Van Gogh's,
that I thought were crows but now know,
because of their plurality, were rooks.

And yes, there were bloodstains.
You'd be surprised at the price of an orange pressé.

MICHAEL HENRY

Ducking and Diving

and everything beyond bends down
going where your head is going
    Montale: from *Cuttlefish Bones*

I loved to chink sapphire glass beads weighting down a lacy
    cloth over Nan's milk jug
then suddenly see them lit turquoise by sun draining colour
    from my hand, melting
gold chenille and creamy linen . . . flaming Tizer moving like a
    sunset across pink & black
comic strips, ogling through rising bubbles Desperate Dan
    chasing a cow-pie,
flicking sugar crystals from my lips, swallowing jam bursts
    from a doughnut, while
two lilac hyacinths, stoic in a grey windowbox among chimney
    pots, glow like a resurrection:

Nan's beloved Bess, a curly blackhaired two yr old, the white
    sail of her pinafore
flying like a Lowry stick-girl in a fall from a ladder left
    against the yard wall;
my great-grandfather, sinking under a failing business, going
    down in a suicidal leap
disguised for the Insurance Man by a pail and cloth left on
    the sill like an
exchange, as if he had just slipped backwards from a missed
    gesture in a goodbye wave,
all the steps & black railings out front that could have speared
    him, marching to Portobello;

Mum a fleeting shadow among market stalls rampant with bright
        cloths and ribbons,
barrowboys' amazing tricks, balancing a dinner service in a crazy
        fan along one arm,
then leaning extravagantly to charm housewives who turn a rueful
        smile, the taste of shell-
fish from a tiny porcelain dish Dad's hand is lowering & tipping,
        the corner shop baking
its loaves over & over again in late sun above a black grille
        where Mum as a girl
marched on steam to keep warm, like downward rushes of heat
from
        red buses on a cold morning;

moored chickens in the sweetshop's back yard where, as a friend,
        I was let under
a trapdoor in the counter, crouching through portals of darkness
        smelling of cloves & liquorice
and everything from the back of beyond bending down going
down
        where my head is going.

RITA CARTER

Field of Snowdrops

I thought I'd missed the snowdrops but no,
there they were, drooping in unexpected banks
like the war cemeteries I visited
with my parents in Northern France.

If I could be at my mother's skirts again,
those skirts that draped better when I was small,
clipping with the tiniest, shiniest scissors
the uneven tassels of the sofa's shawl.

Those scissors, confiscated, never to be seen again.
They could have cut the snowdrops as they massed
or in the cemeteries of France
straightened a tiny fringe of grass.

MICHAEL HENRY

Salt Islands

Winter was the landscape of my island:
bitter winds, late afternoons, the wet brash
of salt and rain flaying me, making my skin sing.
I was afloat in my father's isolation,
held on the surf side of his other island,
pinned furthest from the road that led away
and now leads back again.

I was not the only one to notice
the process of the storm's diffusion
as water and the skyline become one,
odd days, storms cutting clean across horizons
until the calm (as it always did)
stitched it together. Fine scars.
Continual separation, suspension, division.

There were balmier days, hotter summers
than these now are, earlier mornings wading
as the tide was turning in my favour.
It was safe then. And later evening
immersions, buoyed by the same salt
only sighing, while tiny silver fish
flashed around me, luminescent, strange, silent.

Now the sound of the sea when I hear it
comes like my head is laid on his chest
as it was in the beginning and at the end.
Salt still drives the back of my throat.
The island lies in Winter, permanent,
while, inland, gulls remind me that water
is never far away on an island.

TRICIA TORRINGTON

Slow Black Car

Perform a slow
              chassé
                        now pause
click back to
    my house
            set back
      in shadow
like a child's drawing
            a lone cloud
                buckling its panes
hold   dumb air   resurrecting itself
    sky rolling up
      bluer
              a rare cerulean
through wingmirrors   guardian angels
forging ahead
              in star dazzles
      stare out through
      their twin sights
             a soldier on parade
feel the street
through my back
              ghosting the hollow
between my shoulder
              blades

the car ahead
      its shawled
             rear window's glare
    scissored
in black shadows   flower petals vibrating
over the back wheel
    hub cap   whose swerving
                convex mirror

    shatters
                        then clears
    bending concrete
        lamp posts   into a curve
            of dinosaur heads

    wavering shut gates
        & trees
                              twisting
                        pavements
    to a vanishing
        point
    rippling a neighbour
                      standing
    between curtain
        slabs
                    the O
    of his mouth
               silent

RITA CARTER

Evening Diary

The sultry weather's cloud of gnats
means a crop of red bites in bed tonight.
The peeling walls support the usual
skittering brood of attic mice.
Hawks squeal and glide as their young ones learn
how to find food in the fields below
or float to the hill fort above,
flies crowd the window as my fingers tap
and words show up on the screen
in this watchtower cabin of a workplace,
and the bloodshot globes, tomatoes
that glow and fall in the greenhouse
and the dying fabric of summer flowers
are the closing act of the drama in which you shone.
The continuing lives have lost their essence
now with your slow decay.
Your carcass mourns
the lost vibrancy. The air is stifling.

I dare not recall
your fragmented soul at the time you left
with your blank expression, the deep,
deep chasm that was once your understanding, no longer
telling day from night, no longer caring
that you could not comprehend, nor feeling
the least torment in the last slough of your long decay.
Instead, the image that keeps on rising
belongs to the gentle one who worshipped the hills,
created beauty in quiet hours, and loved.
The fir tree's needles are dense and black,
the weathercock stays unmoving and unmoved,
even the selfish creeper has eased its growth
and the small birds stay silent, hours on hours.

Come quickly, death, in a spirit of mercy,
complete the work you began before ever we knew,
defy the fears of the moralists,
let him peacefully free, out of his prison
into his place in the universe.
Come quickly, however you loosen his chains.
I did all I could, God knows: the place
where they took him is harsh and stark with endless
purposeless wandering through its spaces,

inexplicable cries of sudden rage,
the tight-lipped carers, frightened callers,
bodies that linger, dead hope that defies.

Those who preach only
on life and death and nothing between
—what do they understand?
Less than the earthworm slowly toiling
in its underworld task to serve us all.
The red leaves that you loved, the sculptured stump,
the wave-pattern of hills, the composting mound
warm in these last summer evenings
unite with my heart as you sink into sleep
and winter draws nearer, the long dark hours,
the promise of far-off spring.

JOHN HARRISON

In the Arboretum

I walked here as a girl, winter and summer,
always either very hot or very cold.
Nothing mediocre about childhood.
And here I was again, laying down memory

like these trees adding rings, and still
the rose eludes me, your vision building.
A bud opens out, layers peel away and we
are palms up, open mouthed, gasping for air

nothing between us. We share it all,
strip and layer, strip and layer, but you
would not treat a tree like this: no.
Careful! We're in rare times, like stonemasons

who never lived to see their great cathedrals,
and here, laid out years ago, stubs and buds
some kind of foundation followed by
the stop-start of growing. It's hard, this

occasional loving, where the pain comes:
no names carved, but someone will visit,
divine from the rings in a full-grown bud
winter, summer, drought, frost, flood.

AMANDA ATTFIELD

Winter Flowering Jasmine

Given a high wall
and enough winters to scale it,

a century, perhaps,
of runnels and frost-cracks,

it will skitter down
in its own spray,

dancing stars to left
and right, soft

powdery-yellow stars,
first flower of the world,

innocent as the day
is young.

ROGER GARFITT

A Bloom of Light

We inhabit the dark
waiting for the light
to retrieve us

to that point & balance
of the dawn

where silver irradiates
all the known & loved things
into their own shining

a window frame
dirty panes smudged emblazoned

an empty milk bottle
filled with a bloom of light

that sense of overbrimming
sweetness that lightens
a room

your hand dissolving
the chill between my shoulder blades.

RITA CARTER

Muses hard to find

Go one better than Dali does,
commit his droopy watches
into the cracking flames.

Burn the grandfathers, cackle away
at crackle and hiss succeeding
to their ponderous tickings.

Dance bolder yet about your pyres,
igniting Greenwich, solemn place,
go torch Big Ben itself.

Go after timelessness. Aid me,
redundant, outworn Father Time.
Do it now. Drop your scythe.

BRYAN PODMORE

Georg Trakl
1887–1914

Trakl grew up in Salzburg, the 'beautiful city' of his poems that was a shadow of what it once had been. He saw himself as a *poète maudit* in the manner of Baudelaire, whom he sought to emulate even in his addictions.

In 1914 he was sent to Galicia as a lieutenant in the Medical Corps. After the battle of Grodek, he was left in charge of ninety seriously-wounded men whom he was unable to help. One of them shot himself through the head. Trakl became suicidal himself and was removed to Cracow, where he took an overdose of cocaine.

It was Rilke who saw that Trakl's poems were not a record of his state of mind but an intense response to the world, expressed through an original and sustained use of colour. Black may be the colour of death and decomposition but it is also the colour of footsteps and frost, of rain and tears.

MICHAEL HENRY

Grodek

At nightfall the autumn woods cry out
With deadly weapons and the golden plains,
The deep blue lakes, above which more darkly
Rolls the sun; the night embraces
Dying warriors, the wild lament
Of their broken mouths.
But quietly there in the willow dell
Red clouds in which an angry god resides,
The shed blood gathers, lunar coolness.
All the roads lead to blackest carrion.
Under golden twigs of the night and stars
The sister's shade now sways through the silent copse
To greet the ghosts of the heroes, the bleeding heads;
And softly the dark flutes of autumn sound in the reeds.
O prouder grief! You brazen altars,
Today a great pain feeds the hot flame of the spirit,
The grandsons yet unborn.

GEORG TRAKL (1914)
Translated by Michael Hamburger
and reprinted with his kind permission.

The Dead Man's Stitch

The whiff of salt, of iodine, of tar,
as the hand with a red fever
sways in his hammock towards death.

Above him in the darkness, the creak
of rigging and the flap of the mainsail
accompanies the sea's relentless theme:
wave and wind.

Below decks there is half-heard movement,
the lighting of clay pipes,
and the loud, rough accents of seamen
as, like a spill of fire, the dark rum goes down.

If he could sleep now,
he would dream of town and shire,
faraway in miles and further in years.
He'd catch up his brothers as they begin
another golden harvest, reclimb the tall tree
he imagined was a galleon's mast
when first the ocean welled in his blood.

The morning gathers itself, the sun's eye rises
over the great plain of waters.
Silently death has come aboard.
Tough thread is taken up and a grim needle.
The ritual sewing will turn hammock into shroud.

Someone is ordered to fetch cannonballs.
Two are placed inside, down at the feet.
Finally, *The Dead Man's Stitch*; the needle slips through
the bridge of the nose: no twitch or flicker,
a last confirmation of the soul's departure.

The crew are restless and afraid.
They busy themselves to forget; no one says much.
The day will seem long:
blue waves, white waves, green waves
and a storm brewing to westward.

CHRISTOPHER ALLAN

Poem for Owen

I still feel diffident about rummaging through her things
but the wooden box fell off the mantelpiece in her bedroom
and inside among the cuttings was a photograph of Owen
who died two weeks after arriving in France.
His face was beautiful, as finely chiselled as I remembered
seeing the picture as a child
so when I stood for the two minutes silence
it was always his face I saw
as though he represented all the young men
who might have been.
I do not have a living male relative
but he always looked as though he would have been my friend.
He didn't meet me but he met my sister.
He would rush into the kitchen calling
'Where's the baby? Where's the baby?'
and pick her out of the pram to throw her in the air
till she screamed with laughter and Mother shouted
'Owen, Owen, be careful! You'll drop her.'
So this beautiful boy, who loved babies,
I do not think he would be a natural killer
or a good soldier. I think he didn't stand much chance.

MIRANDA TITE

The Ripple Effect

What were the words of that poem you liked
forty years ago in Vienna?
I can only remember incidentals:
the pebble-grey slacks of our tutor,
his *swarfega* black hair
and the white belt that he always wore.
How passionately we debated capital punishment
and how he clinched it with the words: '*Judicial error.*'
Nor will I forget the Greek student who tried
to slip you off my shoulder like a coat.

Under the awnings of green umbrellas
fishermen sit in dark confessionals.

I throw a pebble into the rosebay window of the lake
and watch the ripples.
That is all I ever do. Watch the ripples
long after the stone has disappeared
into the black water. And you too.

MICHAEL HENRY

Lament

Soft are the pine needles.
A cold wind is blowing,
pigeons coo and a dog barks in the distance.

Sentries of creamy narcissus sway
and raspberry rhododendrons
cluster like sweets.

Where will I hide from your death?
In the brown broken bracken,
in the fragile fringes of pine forest,

down the stream-riven valley,
along the ridges of blue-wreathed
wooded hills,

where from smoky skies
gold is breaking.

Riveting an almost dry stone wall,
waterfalls of sapphire and purple heliotropes
are eclipsed at the end
by a spray of snowdrops

like a moon-clip

a cuticle
lighting your little finger
on the edge of your
death.

RITA CARTER

Queuing with Trakl

While I'm waiting I can admire the daffodils,
while I'm waiting I can listen to the birds panting,
while I'm waiting I can smell the perfumes of herbs,
while I'm waiting I can be glad of a damp brick shed
falling in on itself, while I'm waiting
I can go with the donkeys who think they are horses
who think they are camels who think they can fly,
while I'm waiting I can hold on to what I haven't got.

> *He applied to join a lonely hearts club*
> *but they replied they weren't that lonely.*

While I'm waiting I can enjoy the hills in the distance,
while I'm waiting I can play at rearranging words.

> *Did you know about the man who shot an arrow*
> *into the air—and missed?*

While I'm waiting I can pick up the tune coming
down the line, while I'm waiting I can do a bit of
landscape gardening, while I'm waiting I can
clean the windows and polish the floor and
put the kettle on.

> *Nobody knows a poet is alive until they're dead.*

While I'm waiting I can deny the slaughterhouse,
while I'm waiting I can enjoy the terrible privilege
of despair,   so that when Spring says one thing—

> *I told my psychiatrist I had suicidal tendencies*
> *and he said, 'From now on you can pay in advance.'*

While I'm waiting I can deny the reality of the queue,
while I'm waiting I can pick my nose,

> *What do you say when you meet God and he sneezes?*

While I'm waiting I can pretend the queue is for me alone,
while I'm waiting I can notice the Forget-me-nots,
while I'm waiting I can crowd closer to those ahead of me and
to those following, while I'm waiting I can smile for cameras,
while I'm waiting I can sunbathe in black-blue light.

DAVID HART

In Memoriam Georg Trakl, 1887-1914

1. *After The November Poet*

Beneath the facade of the beautiful city
the rats are loose and scuttling for carrion.
The dark moon screams with lived horror.

Away. There are other cities we have in mind.
Redress the balance. My black angel sings.
There are ages behind us. See the fleets of blue

boats, blue flowering souls, hunting eternity
on earth. Have you built yours? Christians
were scared of the wild forest, the city of God.

We're building. We must be. Don't laugh as
the wild man, the innocent idiot, enters singing
of paradise not lost. They went into the dark

early, with hanging corpses, deserters decaying
and putrefied. The dark animals don't quite follow.
The ghosts of the killed are sighing, lamenting.

Wild wolves have broken through the gates.
A dead child walks; the unborn are crying. I
want to be one of the cavalry. My white boat waits

not in Venice: the antechamber of hell. Try Jerusalem
also on our grassed hills. We're building a city where
all can choose to flower, green spirits, blue souls.

2. *The Beautiful City*

I, too, have an obsession with cities.
Women help build them. The rats scurry
like black angels from place to place.

Who can repay the horrors of the past?
Stragglers fall and putrefy. It's not just
romantic melancholia or building a blue ship

for the soul. Imagined communities are where
we live also—not as golden birds descanting
or dusky eagles that gather for slaughter.

Come gently into the light. You flame also.
Your words will sing of the future. A white
angel prays by the waters. Christ is dead

again. We'll build something better. We
have to. See the lights shining like beacons
over the hills. The cities are burning. Imagine

we're marching there together, so we'll build
from dark and light a new Jerusalem in sane
imagined communities, wild men, wild women.

3. Cathedral City in the Nineties

(i)
It is raining
a clear clean
rain. In this
lost city, of Aztec
sacrifice, of gold
worship, it is
raining ... and it
will not wash away
the scars, the poor,
the needs, the system
that splinters and
cannot right itself.
Who do you
worship, fool? It
is a fresh clean
cold rain, with
a hint of fire
coming, in the veins.

(ii)
There is torture
in these prison
camps. They say
the spirit survives.
These holy fools
who want all to
survive, to heal or
not, be happy. In
mud camps and tribes
they called them mad
and listened. In these
prison camps, there is
blood on the wires,
a tapping on the pipes
and veins. The gas ovens

are full again. What
will survive? Gold,
bones, ash, hope.

    (iii)
Planet earth keeps
turning. It sprouts
birds, wind, water.
Moorhens shepherd
their blind young. The
rain comes, and wind
in the middle of summer.
We have our ceremonies.
We have our sacrifices.
Poison seeps into
the drains, the services.
I dream of Nicaragua,
another lost country, and
of Rome in its heyday, and
all the gold of Byzantium.

TREVOR INNES

O Painswick

O Stroud, o Nailsworth
you can be heartbreaking
hills, blindfolded horses
in fields going steep to the
mill river valley
where we no longer find
the mythic piano factory.

Lost through the muddy woods.
Gunshops, bookstall just there
for me to find
Rilke, Kafka, and how
to heal my life,
treat my heart more kindly.

Wooden plates with landscapes
that flow across them
and seas in the sky.

CHARLES JOHNSON

Osip Mandelstam
1891–1938

Mandelstam was one of the great generation of Russian poets who lived through the Revolution. He welcomed it but was dismayed when it was hijacked by the Bolsheviks. His Stalin poem was never published and only spoken among friends, one of whom must have betrayed him. His poems only survived his death in a labour camp because his wife Nadezhda and the poet Anna Akhmatova undertook to memorize them. Nadezha's memoirs of their final years, *Hope Against Hope* and *Hope Abandoned* are well worth seeking out.

ROGER GARFITT

We are alive but no longer feel the land under our feet,
you can't hear what we say from ten steps away,

but when anyone half-starts a conversation
they mention the mountain man of the Kremlin.

His thick fingers are like worms,
his words ring as heavy weights.

His cockroach moustache laughs,
and the tops of his tall boots shine.

He is surrounded by his scrawny necked henchmen,
and plays with the services of non-entities.

Someone whistles, someone miaows and another whimpers,
he alone points at us and thunders.

He forges order after order like horseshoes,
hurling them at the groin, the forehead, the brow, the eye.

The broad-breasted boss from the Caucasus
savours each execution like an exquisite sweet.

OSIP MANDELSTAM (November 1933)
translated by Richard & Elizabeth McKane
and reprinted from *The Moscow Notebooks*
by kind permission of Bloodaxe Books.

String Theory

I

Somewhere in the distance there's a bell
calling faintly, and it's hard to tell
if it's for school or church.
Ahead stretch cupolas of blue and gold,

under my hands a simple wooden gate.
And I am a vibration, a string of sound.
What subtle shift in the song
will make this gate my hand,

my ten fingers its five bars,
turn me gold and blue?
What frequency do we need to be
this earth, this sky?

We can't hear the bell now,
can't go back, can't touch holy water.
We're in too deep for absolution,
too far from the bell's call.

II

And too much is uncovered in this archaeology.
Years of silt sucked away. Eels live in us now.
Dolphins fly about our ruins, salmon shed their scales.

We try to catch them and lose limb after limb
reaching out to the falling rainbow,
to the last great desperate display.

I'm pleading now. Don't see the marble
we were once. Have mercy, let the worms loose,
let them cover us again. And they say

all things come from song. So hum away,
you ancestors, so that here, thirty metres down,
we'll be more than the echoless thud of a dead bell,

more than a dull hammer, beating on stone.

AMANDA ATTFIELD

Two poems in response to Mandelstam's

1. *Iconogram*

Don't look now but the ship of state
is rolling from side to side in its dry dock.
The supports on either side
are rotting and rusting, the prosthetic sticks
of the white Christ dug into the cliffside
are wavering
where the path is circular and signposted
to nowhere.
     The foghorn can't be heard
in the elocution of daylight,
    the semaphore can be seen
waving to itself in the twilight,
    the lookout
puts the tired words to weary music
and reports miracles. The ship of state,

have you noticed, in dry dock
just about weathers the flip-chart storms?

2. *The exile of the imagination*

Now that the sky has become loose-fitting,
now that robins lay parrot eggs,
now that paperclips climb trees,
now that the gravedigger pretends to be a florist
and the priest runs a pawn shop,
anything can be said
without fear of imprisonment:
   the barn roof is falling in on the sour milk,
   the scabby banners are eating the grass,
   roses in their windowless cages are blooming riotously,

while in the planetarium in my head
   —I supply free tea and biscuits—
an unsingable longing
bounces from star to star,
from planet to planet,
dragging faint prayers.

DAVID HART

The Stricken Statesman

When was it that two thousand cheers
surged through proud walls and pillars
to the square, the city, the land?
Gone are the summers of crowds that sang
of adoration: his lips speak words
he has not chosen. His throat has dried.

Once he ran Empire, drove battles
and burned like the fires of his mills.
Now, in his gothic palace of dreams,
entrance hall to the mausoleum,
his head droops humbled, hushed for ever
in a sarcophagus, his chair.

In his park it is winter: the field are dry
and ice overpowers all creeping life.
Only the robin sings of the spirit
that is rootless now, yet finds no outlet
from his carved and gilded walls,
from the ruins of his polished skills.

JOHN HARRISON

Two ups and a down

in homage to Mandelstam

1. Old Times

A trapped moth batters against cracked glass.
This isn't Stalin's Russia. But on the spirit level
dark forces still war. Wasted lives.

My head aches. Dismantle some of the heritage.
Keep a clear space for the best to survive.
The doves return from terror to the apple tree.

2. A Temporary Home

I am at home with the mad and terrified also.
We disappear into black holes. We forget our names
and time. Curtains and carpets bloom like vegetation.

Underworlds are in us, their weeds and snails. Shamans
call from the wilds of Asia, grand-dukes in Mittel
Europa. I wake to a moment which others invade.

Bullies switch into their sinister mode. Should I
master their phrases? Terrors form on telly.
There are pilots in the dark. It can't be a crime to want

a woman who'll heal me and still love me when I'm strong.
I've seen blades on footpaths, nearly driven into trees.
The world reverberates disaster. Some seem happy. I'll float

with them one day. I have antennae which should send, not just
receive. I want to walk proud within the larger worlds
around us sharing the load of the ages like an ark.

3. Sorry, No Alternative

This is a fine and fair
preparation for hell:
take a human being, any

old one will do. Strip
everything he could believe
in, piece by piece: home,

family, justice, a city, nature's
balance, a country, hope. And
love, make sure that disappears.

Then gloat over their destruction.
Only an android after all,
lower class at that. Peel off

the skin, disentangle the fibres,
polish up the scars, dissect and
tear with your knives every

piece that might still be human.
Then set him wagging and
smiling, on the backseat of the car,

locked in a windowless room.
And we are the glory of this world,
like this, as we are, this city, its glory.

TREVOR INNES

Draw no conclusion

the parallels are too easy
and the comparisons are dubious
if not actually smelly.

A friend in Finland
went for years to Russia
buying clocks, selling them
in the auction houses
of Western Europe and Chicago
'without'—'as his passport said—
'let or hindrance' from state
or mafia.

He doesn't go now:
simply too dangerous
—and he speaks of a desire
on the streets for a return
to the order and certainties
of previous systems.

* * *

Dining one night in Lyme Regis
(in a restaurant we should have left)
we fell into conversation
with another marooned couple
come down from Ringwood
within scent of
recently liberated mink.

A few of these creatures
had legged it into the woods
to enjoy—or not—
a fugitive existence.
Others stopped at the main road,
not knowing how to cross.
Most, when breath or nerve
ran out, simply stopped, turned
and made their way back
to the gates, minkly whimpering
to be let in and fed.

We finished our meal,
said thanks for the company
and the story,
and returned meekly
to the order
of the caravan park.

RICHARD BEAUMOND

Label

When she was born
it was there. It did not come
away with the placenta.

Her firm root gripped down,
a strong fist
anchored in darkness. She

felt she'd grow and spread,
lifting pink hands
towards the sky's bowl.

But something lay prone
along her shoulders,
marking her out.

Glinting in sunlight,
silver blades would close
on her, defining limits.

This pruning meant survival,
yet in their very freedom
do not wild flowers thrive?

She was trained across
a trellis, colourful yet tagged,
caged by a mere word.

CHRISTOPHER ALLAN

Derek Walcott
born 1930

Derek Walcott is an exemplary figure for contemporary poets because he had to forge his poetry out of unrecognized materials, giving a voice to the dispossessed. He was born on St Lucia in the West Indies, where he was slightly set apart, a Methodist on a Roman Catholic island, a teacher's son, reared on 'Pears Cyclopedia', growing up among people who spoke a French *patois*. But beneath those differences lay a deeper displacement, in which everyone shared. As an Afro-Caribbean, he was born to a profound, if intangible, sense of exile, to

> some open passage that has cleft the brain,
> some deep, amnesiac blow.

All sense of origin lost when they were uprooted by slavery, his people had to subsist in the margins of another nation's history, seeming to have no place in the language.

With so much cause for anger, it is instructive to see how his voice has grown through tenderness. Walcott can be a hard-hitting satirist and, as the director of a theatre company, he had to engage as closely with the ironies of independence as he had with the conflicts of colonialism. But he began as a painter and gradually, as he came to realize that he was 'powerless, except for love', he has returned to the painter's instinct for celebration. 'Omeros', for which he was awarded the Nobel Prize in 1992, is a celebration on an epic scale of the 'benediction' and the 'particular pain' of his native island.

There is an alchemy in Walcott between the private and the public poetry, the losses of the personal poems seeming to deepen and inform the public voice. There is also, in a body of work built up over fifty years, a reflection on the changing perspectives of age, and it was this that seemed to spark off some of the poems written in the workshop.

ROGER GARFITT

For no one had yet written of this landscape
that it was possible, though there were sounds
given to its varieties of wood;

the *bois-canot* responded to its echo,
when the axe spoke, weeds ran up to the knee
like bastard children, hiding in their names,

whole generations died, unchristened,
growths hidden in green darkness, forests
of history thickening with amnesia,

so that a man's branched, naked trunk,
its roots crusted with dirt,
swayed where it stopped, remembering another name;

breaking a lime leaf,
cracking an acrid ginger-root,
a smell of tribal medicine stained the mind,

stronger than ocean's rags,
than the reek of the maingot forbidden pregnant women,
than the smell of the horizon's rusting rim,

here was a life older than geography,
as the leaves of edible roots opened their pages
at the child's last lesson, Africa, heart-shaped,

and the lost Arawak hieroglyphs and signs
were razed from slates by sponges of the rain,
their symbols mixed with lichen,

the archipelago like a broken root,
divided among tribes, while trees and men
laboured assiduously, silently to become

whatever their given sounds resembled,
ironwood, logwood-heart, golden apples, cedars,
and were nearly

ironwood, logwood-heart, golden apples, cedars,
men . . .

DEREK WALCOTT: 'Homage to Gregorias' Chapter 8 III
from *Collected Poems 1948–1984*.
Reprinted by kind permission of Faber & Faber

Dialect Words

For an hour or more now, the scrape
of a shovel in the cellar
setting slack free,
sending coals skedaddling
down the slope.

Ankle deep in them, they won't
keep still. Let them bite
with their gritty little teeth.
Sneck, beck, gozzle, snitch, laik:
they're spiky with throat sounds.

Scrubbed, you can suck them,
taste them hard, cold and dark
as a pit or the North Sea with
its Viking trails. They snap
into a diamond wash.

Like moon.
Moon that is rock and metal
turns into milk washing across
the ocean floor of a bedroom
239,000 miles away from itself.

BRENDA LEALMAN

Great North Road

for Rhiannon

Sung into day by small birds
I saw Llanyre through early haze
lit up like a headlamp
beamed into morning by a sun
over my shoulder, behind the ridge
and I want to make this journey.

Not Runcorn coiled in its own steam
nor the ship canal oozing from the city's sump
but east of the sun, west of the moon,
over the hills and far away,
the diesel's ground bass
thrumming through the wheel
running down horizons.

Today you are my true North
your lodestone pulling me round,
this untaken journey—

like the car's shadow reaching ahead—

to you

GAVIN HOOSON

Annabel & Anthony

Annabel is tall, straight and seems to rise
as she comes towards me in pale mauve jeans,
dark Hellenic curls around her ears
like a Sybil from a frieze.

Her voice is talking through an oracle
calling through trees, hemmed in natural caesuras
like a breath before a wave;

her hooded blue gaze steady as an eagle's,
her opening palm a petiole in her readiness
to assume that what she is saying
I will fulfil.

There are four walls that break into a sweat
in the atrium where patients come & go
dreaming of what their given symbols resemble,

or stop, remembering another name
near to a sign: PUT YOUR STUBS IN THE BIN
chalked in red on blue slate,

the jade & white striped parasols
bracing in the wind.

On a day bright with traffic
the ghosts were lifting with light hands
my son falling through space

and Anthony is rocking & circling
his calf & foot that is crossed over
the other at an increasing pace

and nodding his blond cropped head,
an Olympic calm on his long forehead
and deep-set blue-grey eyes
that resemble Alexander the Great,
a conqueror come home

even though he speaks with a gargle
though so clearly now when I lean
to greet him with a kiss
and whisper that I know what
he did, and he is telling me

that after jumping off the carpark roof
he met my late son falling through air
occupying the same wound of immense emptiness
when the sky was a blue lake
and the air bright with traffic

like an upside-down reflection.
They fell right through Roland
who is now crossing from one chair
to another as I unclasp my locket

like a wave and he declares
clear as a bell
to the photo, crying out its name,
'Yes—that is Tom when he is sixteen,'
as if he were here and well again

and it goes through me like a knife
as I listen to Bowie
singing *Star Man* . . . 'the stars are in his blood'
and I am one with everybody
on the terracotta sofas
that smell of rust

this Mayday afternoon
the billiard table bald
except for one white ball & a cue left
at an angle, sharp as a Hockney painting,
and every now & then, evenly spaced,

a moan floating down from an upstairs
window outside where, bouncing a ball, a man
gets three baskets in a row in the atrium

and the thin profile of the old lady
leaning forward to catch the film,
a grainy black and white flick,

while bright forks fall through the air,
my younger son Nick eating his belated lunch
like a starving man, working his own cure
gulping cup after cup of orange—

Days, days, the sun
thrumming, thrumming
into the temples
and the old lady leaning forward
with such grace & precision
along the sofa's edge

like a figurehead on a ship
that is ploughing out to sea
its cargo of sufferings,

creaking, tightening
with the rigging of pink blossom.

RITA CARTER

Retreat

i

We are not yet easy with the new dawn chorus:
slamming doors, starter motors, the milk float's whine,
thumps and the shower running in the floor above,
the steady traffic groan, and the metronomic throb
of music from Tamsin and her boyfriend below.
Time for tea in bed, to skip the sales-driven headlines
that exaggerate disputes and call them 'fury';
instead, go through the weekend plan: lunch with Jean,
Chloe's birthday party, Guys and Dolls at the Rep,
then Sunday at the new arts centre by the Park.

Strange they are gone, the Arcadian years
of two-faced retreat, that suburban graft
on rootstock of country, our seduction
by the curves of hills, beeches and alders,
even the heavy grey days that could break
into brilliance without warning, like one
late evening in spring with passing walkers,
blackcap and chiffchaff calling, a whitethroat
stopping briefly, sunlight through young green leaves.
With our closest friends and miniature Kew
we were content, as at leisure we sought
the shy pale flowers of identity.

How will you manage? What will you do? Those questions
again, after twenty years. The last day we called
on Dave Jones, the neighbour still housebound, his farming
lifetime in pictures, six on his living room walls.
That night at the George was the bowling club party.
A score of goodbyes, last one of all to the lane,
swallows gathering for flight on the wires above.
Rival voices still whispered, but the tribe had called
and our plans were laid out years ago, to return
to the city that forged us, to which we owed all.

ii

For decades we had longed
for quiet among fields,
for time to hear the tongues
in trees, to read at ease

a new uncluttered page,
to understand the passions
of the lean and slippered age
unrecognized, unsung.

We dared to take the apple
of the self-knowledge tree
at home above the ripples
of a river, running free,

yet knew that we must still
see through others' eyes,
even there, beneath the hills,
if we would be wise.

Now, like the Duke and all his friends,
we are back with the envious court.
And the yellow leaves of the trees by the flats
quiver, as though this were Arden.
The clouds of time move close above us,
the roots of pleasure are under threat
from the seventh age of man,
but for us, perhaps, the ripened fruit
will be loveliest in drought.

Only Jaques stayed in Arden.

JOHN HARRISON

Old

I am imprisoned in an old man's bones.
I walk his walk
and when it's very bad
I think his old man thoughts.

I walk in rain now.
The rain is talking loudly in the tree.
A larch has fallen in big chunks
across the track.

I must step high
or stop.

MIRANDA TITE

Mingus: Self-Portrait in Three Colours

Not that he glances out of it, he is glancing away,
even the colours are glanced away, doubt overlays them
so that they are fired and burn back through the glaze,

anemones on a cafe table, arranged in a liturgy of love,
all the colours of blood against the small check of the cloth,
the blue has a premonition, there is an inkling in the red,

but the magentas pulse as they darken, still in flood,
searches rather than colours, chances of the light
as it runs the length of its wave, split seconds that give

the only glimpse of him.

ROGER GARFITT

People Carrier

These are the people carriers of Africa.
Full to bursting, *standing room only*,
men riding pillion on the running boards.

They drop through the well of Africa,
chunder up clouds of dust on dirt roads,
parade in triumph through the cities
like Caesar regnant.

Float by carnival float streams past.
We can hear the rattling tins
and throw our good wishes in.

There are no straps to hang on to,
no thought of what comes after,
only foot hard down on the accelerator.
This is the bandwagon that Africa's on.

MICHAEL HENRY

Rabindranath Tagore
1861–1941

Tagore is the most widely translated Indian writer of all time. His English translation of his *Gitanjali* won the Nobel Prize in 1913 and influenced writers all over the world. In the *Gitanjali* he uses the lover as an image for the divine and I asked the workshop to extend this idea, retelling a fairy story or a folk tale as an allegory of the search for the divine. The epigram was another way of thinking for Tagore and we started by writing some epigrams of our own.

DEBJANI CHATTERJEE

The Unknown You Have Made Known

The unknown you have made known to me,
    In so many homes you gave me shelter.
You have brought the distant near, my friend,
    And made a brother of the stranger.

        I fear to leave a place I know of old,
            Who knows what the future will unfold?
        I forget the simple truth that within
            The new, you are the familiar.
        You have brought the distant near, my friend,
            And made a brother of the stranger.

In life, in death, in the far flung world,
    Whenever, wherever I roam,
O Knower of my every birth,
    It is you who will make all known.

        With you, no one can be a stranger.
        There can be no fear, no barrier.
        Your spirit moves us to unite.
            May I have sight of you forever.
        You have brought the distant near, my friend,
            And made a brother of the stranger.

RABINDRANATH TAGORE
translated by Debjani Chatterjee

Bullet Point

One of those questions that required notice:
how my father had tried to join the Emergency Medical Service;
how he had failed a flying test at Hooton—his only failure;
how, if our positions had been reversed
and I had been my father's father,
I would have said something epigrammatic:

'We do not have to think meanly of ourselves
for not having been a soldier.
A dove does not think meanly of itself
for not having been a hawk.'

I remember the flocks of white crosses
and the maverick Stars of David he always noticed
and as the late September sun caught each inscription
I thought of the letters my father had accrued:
FRCS, MCh Orth, MD, medical ones
with no bullet points in between.

MICHAEL HENRY

Epigrams after reading Tagore

There are two continents:
woodsmoke and bees.

*

The oak tree showed me
what an acorn is.

*

A rough day by the North Sea:
somewhere out there the wind stops.

BRENDA LEALMAN

The Gift

It was all so long ago I've forgotten
how it started. You seemed to come
from a dream. From somewhere inside me
you eased out a hand, a shoulder, a thigh.

Trees broke through the ground, but
it was as if I'd always known leaves;
then rain gave a shine to your skin
and fruit fitted my palm with a strange exactness.

Later, when I watched you walking away
towards the light, I knew I was hollow.
I crossed the river, climbed a hill
and saw you still drifted beyond me.

Then you turned and opened your mouth
and began to sing. It was
soon after that you stole up on me
surprising me with a gift. What could I do

but hold out my hand to take it?
There it lay, fresh and round and good.
And how sweet it tasted, though the core
was bitter and would bruise my tongue.

Since then, how many red suns have risen
over the land? How many moons
have grown and dissolved, mirroring your cycle?
Now I am old, they dissolve

into each other. Yet my love endures,
even though you now sleep under clay.
I will not let them speak ill of you.
Long ago, what you gave me was the world.

CHRISTOPHER ALLAN

Penelope

So long ago, I cannot remember
when I started to wait for your return.
So long since the war that I wonder
at times whether it happened at all.
No news arrives here but rumour
and tales I dare not believe.
One I can't bear, of a woman
who held you for more than a year
by some sort of supernatural power.
You, great commander? A likely one.
And another about a girl called Calypso
—they say she has lovely hair.
Have all these years of fidelity
been wasted, of no account?

Our family home is now an inferno
of intrigue. Last night I went out
with the usual guards to the lonely
height of the mountain, to gaze at
the facing shore, the harbour below,
the silent, far-stretching Ionian Sea.
As ever, you were not in evidence.
How assiduous they are,
the devils that seem to live in this place.
Our son, who just toddled when you quit,
has a haunted look in his eyes.
Without fail I pray to you each night,
to the gods, to anyone else
who may listen. You are never there.

JOHN HARRISON

Two Epigrams and a Folk Tale

1. Presence

I looked and you did not come.
When I turned away you had gone.

2. Words

If we name you, you'll disappear.
If we don't, you'll still break free.

3. Home Comforts

I walked in all innocence through the wood.
I carried my communion. The gate was open,
the house silent. And then I saw the vision:
no hanging corpse but granny as a wolf.

TREVOR INNES

Hospitality for a silkie

(*Bardsey Island, June 2000*)

'Extra-fine towels, Guestmaster,
we have a visitor with nothing
but the fish-skin he lives in.
He sings plaintively, Guestmaster,
but seems to have no words,
holy or otherwise. He smells of deep water
and snorts when offered beer,
when offered milk,
when offered spring water.
Put him at the head of the table
with the best plate, Guestmaster,
and we will pray for his eternal soul
in the best language we have available
and sweetly.'

DAVID HART

No physics without faith

(*From a sequence written after Aelfric's* The Assumption of Saint John the Divine. *Saint John survived two attempts by the Emperor Domitian to kill him, first by boiling in oil, then by exile on the barren island of Patmos, where he is said to have written the Book of Revelation.*)

He drowns me in a cauldron,
lights touchwood under the vat.
The oil brightens. Water vapour
pebbles the crucible with jewels of air.
I feel its art
sweetening my flesh. Blood, bones
flow like wingbeats, like the voice of rivers,

and I rise, purified.

Blinded by this demonstration
of elementary physics,
the emperor exiles me to Patmos,
waits for hunger, thirst, to finish me.

What do I need, why feed, who am transported?

There's nature—birth, appetite, death—
and there is miracle;
and they are close, close.
Only a net in the mist marks
where air and water meet. I am
the man mending the net.

ELEANOR COOKE

Yehuda Amichai
1924–2000

Yehuda Amichai was born into an Orthodox Jewish family in Bavaria and died in Jerusalem, where he had lived most of his life, some ten days before our October workshop. He developed a new kind of poetry in the Hebrew language, more relaxed, more colloquial, while taking on the big themes of Jewish-Israeli history, religion, and the making of a peaceable future, taking them on with something of an oblique, whimsical eye and ear. The Israeli President and Prime Minister attended his funeral: a poet in Israel has special significance, as a poet does in Wales, where R. S. Thomas had died within a few days of Amichai. We wondered about the significance of poetry and poets in England.

DAVID HART

Like Our Bodies' Imprint

Like our bodies' imprint
Not a sign will remain that we were in this place
The world closes behind us,
The sand straightens itself.

Dates are already in view
In which you no longer exist,
Already a wind blows clouds
Which will not rain on us both.

And your name is already in the passenger lists of ships
And in the registers of hotels,
Whose names alone
Deaden the heart.

The three languages I know,
All the colours in which I see and dream:

None will help me.

YEHUDA AMICHAI: from *Selected Poems* (1971) translated by Assia Gutmann with the collaboration of Ted Hughes and reprinted by kind permission of Penguin Books

To the spirits of this place

Autumn, and I'm rifling the cupboard again,
fingering mythologies for the shadow behind the image—
the god in the hoof print.
I've worn their bones like an amulet.
The man with the power.

But I've never heard the voice,
though bruised with listening.

Out here in the wood I've done it again.
Daring to be disappointed, as usual, I am.

I turn for the house past the cedar's caryatid
go in under a leaf-psalm susurrus.

GAVIN HOOSON

Next Time I Wake in an Empty Bed

Will I recognize the message
you leave if you leave one
hidden somewhere in the flat

an upturned glass

the stem of a white
or purple headed flower
broken perhaps

or a phone number under the pillow

but no name

so I'll stay
at a disadvantage, be wrongfooted
if I ring.

Who's calling?
you'll ask

and I still won't
know who you are.

You must stay until I know
who you are, then stay
because I do.

CHARLES JOHNSON

Messengers

*Words are a new beginning
with the stones of the past*   (Yehuda Amichai)

At the end of summer, in a great hubbub of buzzing
provoked by a noisy wasp, flies are resettling,
warming themselves on the side of the summerhouse,
meandering over a blistered geography of turquoise paint,
flaked, scrolled and fragile as an old papyrus;
slack waves peeling back to reveal
islands of sandy wood
where dark slaves congregate.

Most come to rest in smoother, shiny grooves
between horizontal slats, like climbers
pausing below an overhang, clinging on sideways,
legs commas, wings grey dusty armaments,
while other lazily explore
supporting uprights and sidebeams.

Erased by season or migratory need
they could all fly off randomly
like birds or words
to alight on another page.

In the middle distance near a lake
cows are grazing, moving forward slowly
in trammelled lines, while others keel over,
lying down like stones or boulders
that break in different formations,
reassembling like a rubik cube unpredictably
but with the cipher of an underlying
unvarying frequency.

Urgent in blue sky
a calligraphy of lemon leaves
collapse on to the pale grey decking
of the summerhouse, one pausing lightly
on my notebook; a monarch surfing
a strange attractor, skeletal veins and scallops
arching the politics of dream

while flies crawl the cracks
like messengers
between the stones.

RITA CARTER

Toadstool

I thought it was a toadstool
then I thought it was a fallen leaf,
I turned it over with my foot
and it was a toadstool
and I apologized.

The compensation for the toadstool
is this poem,
except the toadstool can't hear or read it
and even if it could once
its lovely brown head
has been decapitated.

Now the headless toadstool is willy-nilly
becoming a metaphor, out of my control.
I put my hands over my ears
and I close my eyes
but I can't stop it:
> the fickle body politic,
> the earth's finger up to God in the sky,
> the funnel of a ship all but sunk,
> the world tree
> with the roof of the world burned off,
> childhood kicked over.

But, reader, I've been clever with this poem,
haven't I,
turning it this way and that astutely,
making up handsomely
for bending the toadstool's head off with my foot
—and there was no malice in it—
putting on paper something the toadstool
even whole
could never have achieved?

DAVID HART

A boy killed in Palestine

(*in memory of the poet Yehuda Amichai*)

Did you fall in the sand?
Sand! It was rubble—ammunition—
stones to throw to fight a war.
All your young eyes ever saw
before they glazed in death.

Blood dries quickly in the sun.
A mother weeps on the stone steps.
She knows you are in paradise—
learning to play in cool green shade.
Splash in the water—build a dam—
climb the beautiful trees.

Who killed you, child?
Did God hear the wrong prayers?
Did the soldiers not understand?
Should we have gone there to shout 'Stop!'?

Did the poet speak?
What did he say?

URSULA FREEMAN

All Poets are Wounded Men

See that man over there
idling under an apple bough?
He is one of the wounded men.

          You say
you see no blood
run down his sleeve, note
his face is not punctured.

But you notice how his eyes
light a little
like small flames fed by the wind.

Does he have a name, the wounded man?

He has told me names are not important.
He has told me merely to focus
on what is before your eyes,
              moment to moment:
cloud and star,
              hill, briar and beast;
the man feeding his computer
in the high-rise made of steel and glass;
the waiting call-girl
              lovely in a red window;
or the lost child playing alone
in a puddle of petrol.

          Tell me, you say,
where is the wound of the wounded man?

For we have just seen him leave
the cool shadow of the apple tree
and venture a sunlit track
              towards the city.
He does not limp, his pace is even.
He carries nothing in his hands.

          I think his wound
festers somewhere below his heart.
The road he is on is full of ghosts
and so is the wounded man
              and so is the wind.

CHRISTOPHER ALLAN

Mr Amichai

The world is full of people who are going to die, Mr Amichai,
and your turn has come. A blessing I ask then
on your after-death journey, a blessing I ask on your memory,
a *Thankyou*, too, a confused thankyou, an it's-all-done thankyou,

and I see you smiling and frowning at this:
you've written all your poems now, and I'm adding this one,
and you are saying, 'It's not necessary, it's not a good idea at all,
go and enjoy yourself, go for a walk,
talk to the trees, be ready for a surprise,
ask a blessing on all children,
don't hold me up with a poem, let me go.'

And even as I'm working on this poem, R.S., too, has gone.
Did you ever meet, did you read each other's poems?
You can travel together, two old poets of uncertain temper, Jew and
          priest,
Jerusalem and Jerusalem translated into Welsh,
and if you look back, if you will, bless us ambivalently, strangerize us,
in the world still, writing still, still attending workshops,
still thinking of our reputations, still trying to get it right, not yet dead,
not yet taken by the sharp wind.

DAVID HART

Spare the rod

Spare the rod, spoil the child
the saying went, but you had no rod.
Sunday was time for chapel and rest
but the chapel is a furniture store.
Time for bed, you used to say,
and we went, and lay awake.

At the Sunday charity supper
after last weekend in the hills
we knew from labels on the table
the ethics of the food and drink
and toddlers played around our feet.

One day in bed not long ago,
your breathing down to tiny gasps,
you offered your hand.
I still feel your grip, as firm as ever,
and feel the look in your eyes.

JOHN HARRISON

Unsceptr'ing this isle

Hard now to imagine a wedding
without the mother of the bride
standing to read from *The Shortcomings
of a Bridegroom*, the teasing verses
of Madhur Narayan.

Hard to imagine a retirement do
without a singing of *Her Way*,
the seven throws of the Monkey Goddess,
that leave you flat on your back in the dust
at the age of sixty-five.

Harder still to imagine a funeral
without a performance of *The Sheddings*
of Huan Sui, the concluding stillness
as friend after friend of the deceased
enacts a memory into the smoke
of the willow twigs, nine twigs
leant together and lit
in the empty chancel.

ROGER GARFITT

Biographical Notes

CHRISTOPHER ALLAN has a pamphlet, *Dancing in Paper Trousers*, out from Flarestack. Poems in a wide range of magazines, most recently in *Fire*, *Other Poetry*, and *The Rialto*. AMANDA ATTFIELD is a founder member of the Hereford Poetry Group. Poems in a number of magazines, including *The Rialto*. RICHARD BEAUMOND is Arts Co-ordinator at the Community College, Bishop's Castle. RITA CARTER studied at the Royal Academy Schools. She has contributed poems and drawings to all the Border Poets' publications. DEBJANI CHATTERJEE is a poet and translator who has chaired the Translations Committee of the Arts Council of England. Reviews Editor of *Writing in Education*. ELEANOR COOKE has published three collections of poetry, most recently *Secret Files* from Cape. URSULA FREEMAN runs the Redlake Press at Brook House, Clun. ROGER GARFITT's *Selected Poems* are published by Carcanet. He is currently Writing Fellow at the University of East Anglia. CAROLINE GOURLAY's collection, *Against the Odds*, has just appeared from the Hub Press. JOHN HARRISON is a retired doctor living in Bucknell. These are the first poems he has had published. DAVID HART's collection, *Setting the Poem to Words*, is published by Five Seasons Press. He is currently Poet in Residence at the South Birmingham Mental Health NHS Trust. MICHAEL HENRY's third collection from the Enitharmon Press, *Footnote to History*, is about to be published. GAVIN HOOSON works for the Powys County Archive. Poems in *Between the Severn and the Wye*. TREVOR INNES is an Oxford English graduate and retired 6th Form teacher. He lives, paints, and is happily married in Ludlow. CHARLES JOHNSON is joint founding editor of Flarestack Publishing. Poems in *One for Jimmy* and *Beyond Bedlam*. BRENDA LEALMAN was a winner in the 1999 Poetry Business Competition. Two pamphlets out, *Nought at the Pole* from Flarestack and *Time You Left* from Smith/Doorstop. BRYAN PODMORE is Vice-Chair of the National Association of Writers in Education and Associate Editor of *Writing in Education*. GLENN STORHAUG is a poet and translator who specializes in the Scandinavian languages. He is well-known as a book designer and the founder of Five Seasons Press. MIRANDA TITE is descended from a Welsh family who moved their entire farm to Droitwich Spa by train, disembarking in a cavalcade that's remembered to this day. TRICIA TORRINGTON is an artist and photographer and runs a medical research company.